COACH AN
HORSES:
MY STORY IN THE AMBULANCE DISPUTE 1989/90

JOSEPH CONAGHAN

PUBLISHERS
Glantaff House, Troedyrhiw, CF48 4EH

First published in Great Britain 2010

A copy of this book has been lodged at the British Library.

ISBN
978-0-9565482-0-7

Printed and bound in Britain by
HSW Print Rhondda CF40 2XX

Further information including sales

http://josephconaghan.wordpress.com

EDITED BY STEVE DAVIES

CREDITS

Cover Art and Design:	Madeleine Conaghan, Luke Dowson	
Excerpts from Hansard:	With Permission Under Licence	
Parliamentary Licences:	**PSI Licence** number	C2010000317
	Parliamentary Licence number	P2010000056

Acknowledgements:

Steve Davies, Barrie Clement, Bob Abberley, Roger Poole, Ann Mitchell and UNISON for permission to use the COHSE Archive and NUPE publications, Office of Public Service, National Archive, The British Library, Cardiff Library, BMJ, Dave Galligan, Maurice Haslam and Sam Oestreicher (Millar report), Maggie Dunn, Christian Peter Lewis , Kevin Dwyer, Frank Ward, Ron Singh for his extensive research files, Claire Lucas and Peter Gabriel at Real World.

The author would like to give special thanks to the following whose benevolence and kindness have ensured a wider distribution for this book:

Sector members of the 3 UNISON Welsh Ambulance Services branches
A.B.M. University Health Board UNISON branch
Betsi Cadwaladr University Health Board branch of UNISON
West Midlands Ambulance UNISON branch,
South West Ambulance UNISON branch, Cwm Taf UNISON branch,
Gwent Health UNISON branch, GMB Welsh Ambulance branch,
UNISON Cymru/Wales Regional Health Committee,
Liverpool Community and Hospitals UNISON Branch,
Grimsby and Goole Health UNISON branch,
South Central Ambulance UNISON branch

About the author

Joseph Conaghan has worked in the NHS since 1982. He has been a union activist for almost all of his working life - first in COHSE, then NUPE and now in UNISON (into which COHSE and NUPE merged). Today, Joseph chairs UNISON's UK Ambulance Sector Committee. He is also a member of UNISON's NHS Health Care Service Group Executive and the first ambulance member of the NHS Staff Council. He is a State Registered Paramedic.

Joseph has four children ranging from university to nursery age (Madeleine, Isabelle, Grace and James) and lives with his wife, Rhian and three home based children in a village in the South Wales valleys just north of Cardiff

Contents

Introduction by Barrie Clement (based on an interview with Roger Poole)

There has been no industrial dispute like it. Not because of the numbers involved, not because of its direct impact - or even its undoubted political resonance - but because of the degree of support it won from the public.

The conflict between Britain's ambulance staff and the Thatcher government in 1989-90 was over pay, but it paved the way for the "professionalisation" of the job. The ambulance service would never be the same again.

The degree of popular backing it received was illustrated by the millions of pounds collected in buckets by ambulance crews. Rarely, if ever, have members of the public queued to donate money to workers involved in a dispute. Commuters routinely lined up outside London railway stations to express their financial backing. Elsewhere food was donated to crew who were suspended, buses were free and children's toys flooded in during the Christmas of 1989. At one stage pollsters registered more than 80 per cent support for the ambulance staff. The survey was published by the Daily Telegraph, not a newspaper given to enthusiasm for trade unions. Around three-quarters of Conservative voters backed the crews. Even the Sun, Mrs Thatcher's mouthpiece, gave its approval. Some five million people signed a petition in support.

Public sympathy was prompted in large part by the kind of work performed by the employees involved in the dispute. Most people during the course of their lives have cause to be thankful to the care provided by those who work for the ambulance service. Clearly other front-line public servants have a place in the hearts of the public. But not even the nurses - the "angels" beloved of the popular press – had ever experienced such a tsunami of acclamation during an industrial dispute.

The reason for this acclaim, put simply, was that ambulance workers behaved responsibly and were skilfully-led. There was a flexible, carefully-targeted industrial strategy, an absolute determination to maintain unity among the five unions involved and a street-wise approach to public relations. All three combined to give the unions a political edge on a government which had taken on and beaten the praetorian guard of the union movement in the epic miners' strike of 1984-85.

There were five unions involved in the ambulance dispute: the National Union of Public Employees (NUPE), the Confederation of Health Service Employees (COHSE), the National and Local Government Officers' Association (NALGO), the Transport & General Workers' Union (T&G) and the GMB. The first three went on to merge and form UNISON, in fact the solidarity engendered by the dispute convinced COHSE of the need to join the two others in the new organisation. The T&G became part of UNITE.

At one time or another each of these organisations had crossed swords with one another. Each had its individual industrial strategy and political philosophy. Inevitably there had been dispiriting clashes involving egos. In some cases the membership of the unions was very different and had therefore evolved into separate sub-cultures. There were varying attitudes and varying structures. Clashes however were at their worst where unions were competing for the same members.

So if this dispute was going to be successful, the antagonisms would have to be subsumed for the sake of the struggle.

Private meetings of the unions in the late summer of 1989, set the tone for the conflict. It was decided that everyone would sing from the same hymn sheet. The principal national soloist - in fact the only vocalist - would be Roger Poole of NUPE, the union with most members in the service. At local level branch officers were encouraged to talk to journalists about the dispute in their area – although comments on policy were to be left to Roger. The five general secretaries of the unions involved agreed to remain backstage – rarely even venturing into the wings. This was unprecedented.
The unions' high command in the dispute - the so-called "Famous Five" – met fortnightly and was formed from the union side of the Ambulance Whitley Council the negotiating forum. Roger was the spokesman, Bob Abberley of COHSE undertook the job of lobbying MPs, Danny Brien of the T&G chaired meetings while while Donna Covey of the GMB and Owen Davies of NALGO were always on hand and travelled the country addressing meetings of members. Lyn Bryan of NUPE, acted as the main press officer.

It was a tribute to the maturity of the unions that they were prepared to allow Roger to be the front man and to work through one press officer. Over the six months of the conflict Roger, secretary of the union negotiating team, would become a household name. At some stages of the dispute it was virtually impossible to turn on the news on either television or the radio without seeing or hearing Roger. His Bristolian burr became synonymous with ambulance workers and their campaign.

The kernel of the dispute was prosaic – although of high importance to the crews. It was about wages and the restoration of pay parity with the fire service. In 1985 unions had managed to establish parity between trained ambulance staff and firefighters with more than four years' experience – a long-held ambition. Crews gave up shift, weekend, bonus payments and so-called "Spanish practices" in order to secure an all-in salary.

By 1988 however the Government had broken the link with firefighters whose wages were determined by the upper quartile of male manual earnings – a mechanism established after the first national fire strike in 1977. It was a testament to the leadership of Ken Cameron, general secretary of the Fire Brigades Union, that his members had held on to a system which was anathema to Thatcher's ideas of the free market. They were to continue to hold on to it – in no small measure because of the political damage wrought on the Tories by the ambulance workers.
The ambulance dispute was prompted by a 6.5 per cent pay offer at a time when the inflation rate was running at more than eight per cent. It was, in effect, a wage reduction. Ministers had decided that an automatic mechanism was inflationary and that the ambulance service was distinct from the fire brigades - and indeed the police. It was an "essential" service not an "emergency" one and therefore should not enjoy the same arrangements. By 1989 a gap of more than 11 per cent had opened up with their firefighter "comparators". The Advisory, Conciliation and Arbitration Service (Acas) reported at the time that ambulance staff felt they were under-valued and working for a "Cinderella service" being run "on the cheap".

Union officials recommended the offer of 6.5per cent, but ambulance crews rejected it overwhelmingly. Roger said that he was privately aware that it would be turned down. “I was pretty certain that they’d reject it,” he said. “I remembered the Winter of Discontent in 1979 in which good, decent public servants got a hammering from the media. I was absolutely determined that wasn’t going to happen again. I didn’t want senior union officials to lead the dispute, I wanted members to lead the way. If we had put the offer to members with a recommendation to reject, they would have supported their union out of loyalty. I didn’t want a loyalty vote. Members had to be aware that if they rejected the proposals they would be rejecting a final offer. That way nobody could accuse the unions of encouraging members to take on the Thatcher government without their whole-hearted commitment. That gave us a far stronger position, but we knew we weren’t going to get an easy ride from the Tories.”

In fact the Government was gearing up for what they saw as a critical showdown with health service unions in preparation for major reforms, including privatisation. Clarke’s officials reportedly described it as “the miners’ strike for the NHS”.

However the unions were convinced that members should not use the ultimate industrial weapon. “Put simply, if ambulance crews go on strike, people will die. It really is as simple as that. So strikes were out of the question,” said Roger. “We decided that we would maintain an accident and emergency service throughout the dispute. Ambulance men and women wouldn’t have walked out even if we’d asked them to.”
So having rejected offer, the 18,000 union members in the workforce were asked to vote on whether they were prepared to take industrial action short of strikes. The answer was an emphatic Yes. They voted by four to one in favour of taking the Government on. No-one, by the way, was under any illusion that management negotiators were firmly under the ministerial thumb and that ultimately Mrs Thatcher was calling the shots.

At the end of September the crews were joined by their officers and controllers who voted by three to one to join the dispute. NALGO officers and crews met in joint session after that.

“It was quite clear when we started negotiations that the Government was going to be intransigent,” said Roger. “We offered arbitration to settle the argument and said that we would abide by the outcome – even if it came out at 6.5 per cent. We knew, of course, that the Thatcher Government would reject the idea of an independent arbiter, but we needed to show the public that we were reasonable and that we were prepared to compromise. And we were."

Talks yielded nothing of consequence and the action began at the beginning of September 1989 with a ban on overtime. It soon became clear that it was not an effective weapon and it escalated into a work-to-rule. A fortnight later an even tougher line was agreed, with qualified A&E crews refusing to answer non-999 calls. In response to that management docked the pay of those taking the action – and in some areas members were suspended and the Government began to order the army on to the streets to replace ambulance crews

The union replied by declaring that if any members had their pay docked or were suspended, then all members in that service would consider themselves suspended rather than on strike. They would nevertheless continue to provide a 999 service unpaid. "The decision to suspend people was evil. They tried to stop ambulance men and women doing their work," said Roger. At one stage a number of local ambulance services took out injunctions in a bid to prevent employees attending their workplaces and fulfilling their pledge to answering 999 calls.

In an attempt to kick-start negotiations, the unions dropped their demands for a cut in the working week, more holidays and extra pay and holidays for staff with long service. But the Government refused to budge.

"Ministers made it very clear from the outset that they were going to portray us a throwback to the 1970s, to the Winter of Discontent," said Roger. "We had to put a new face in front of the public in an industrial dispute. I was always worried we would end up in the same place as we did in the Winter of Discontent – facing public hostility. It seems to me that it is extremely difficult to conduct an industrial dispute in the public services without public support. But it became quite clear to everyone that we were not a bunch of lunatics and that our aspirations were sensible. The big fear was that somebody would die during the dispute and our members would get the blame. We had to avoid that at all costs."

Roger believes that throughout the conflict, ministers were intent on provoking a walkout so that ambulance workers would lose public backing. Kenneth Clarke,

Secretary of State for Health, took to referring to the crews as "professional drivers", seemingly in an attempt to elicit a militant response.

"The Government did everything to persuade our members to come out on strike. The 'drivers' jibe was part of a concerted campaign to insult our members. We warned our people not to fall into the trap. Overwhelmingly they didn't. They were magnificent throughout." One group in London and another in Liverpool however announced strikes. "That didn't help the dispute, but I understand why they did it. And they were strikes in name only, because they answered serious calls."

Throughout the six months of the conflict, crews stayed on station and gave out numbers to the public so that they could be contacted in an emergency. Staff who had been suspended, routinely attended road accidents where grateful soldiers and police officers often stood aside and let the experts get on with it.

In January in order to assuage growing frustration among crews, the unions called on staff facing management sanctions to refuse calls from managers who were working normally. They would continue to respond however to calls from the police, doctors, hospitals and members of the public.

The high command called on members of the public to show support by stopping work or joining in demonstrations for 15 minutes at midday on 30 January. There was a massive response from workers in both factories and offices. Shoppers throughout the country stood on pavements showing their solidarity. However the unions gave no comfort to ultra-left groups who were calling for a general strike. "They were trying to jump on the bandwagon and turn an industrial dispute into a political dispute with the usual defeat and acrimony that always follows such tactics," said Roger.

The PR battle was fascinating and of critical importance. The Government tried various individuals to "front up" its argument. Apparent differences of opinion inevitably emerged which were interpreted as splits. Among the front men was Duncan Nichol, the NHS chief executive, who had little power to influence the outcome of the dispute. On other occasions it was David Rennie, who chaired the employers' side on the Whitley Council negotiating body.

More often it was Health Secretary Kenneth Clarke - a beer-swilling, superficially affable "bloke" – who was "the human face of the Thatcher Cabinet" – as Roger puts it. But Clarke was no closet left-winger. He was at pains to lose his Nottinghamshire accent when he went up to Cambridge and Roger points out that trade unions were his blind spot. Clarke had identified with the Labour Party in his younger days, but he jumped ship at university.

On radio news programmes especially, Clarke was regularly made to look the bad guy – a persona which was reflected in public opinion polls. The Conservative Party considered appointing a PR minder to hold the Secretary of State's hand. In interviews Clarke seemed to be intransigent while Roger was reasonable; Clarke was authoritarian while Roger was a man of the people. The Cambridge-educated Health Secretary was bested by the clever union official who left comprehensive school at the age of 15 without a qualification to his name.

Mrs Thatcher was viscerally and ideologically opposed to any contact with union representatives - whatever the circumstances. And she had set her face against any concessions to the ambulance workers.

However the lack of contact was almost certainly against Clarke's instincts. Roger and the Health Secretary had struck up a relationship in 1981 at a school where they were debating the proposition that the health service were safe in the hands of the Tories.

Kenneth Clarke knew he was being beaten hands down in the PR battle and he took the opportunity occasionally to defy his mistress by chatting informally and very privately with Roger. One morning the protagonists bumped into each other at the BBC. Roger had been interviewed and was leaving the studio when Clarke walked in.

"He said: 'What are you doing here?' and I replied: 'The same as you but with a slightly different point of view'". Roger was determined to take this chance of speaking to the organ grinder rather than the monkey. After Clarke finished his interview, they walked down the corridor and found an empty room.

"We spent 15 minutes walking round the room saying things like 'what if this happens?' - just trying out different scenarios. Then he suddenly realised where he was and that it wasn't the best place to have a private chat. We were yards away from journalists and television cameras. We had one or two other discussions during the dispute." Mrs Thatcher would have taken a very dim view indeed of one of her Cabinet ministers having informal chats with representatives of the great unwashed. There were also private meetings with Nichols and his colleagues.

The press were keen to test the unity of the five unions by attempting to sniff out splits, but they were precious few. Differences of opinion were kept private. They were subjects of debate at private meetings, but went no further. "One journalist from the (now defunct) Sunday Correspondent called me one Saturday as I was on my way north in a train. He said he understood there was a difference of opinion between me and Bob Abberley. I said it was news to me and I asked him what it was and he was unable to tell me. At least he tried!"

The strategy was to concentrate the PR effort on radio and television, especially the latter. "We wanted out images on the screen, not the Government's. I think we were overwhelmingly successful in accomplishing that." Television coverage of the public service stoppages in the Winter of Discontent was characterised by rat-infested piles of rubbish in the streets. And viewers' screens during the miners' strike were dominated with clashes between police and pickets.

During the ambulance dispute, TV became the crews' best friend with widespread coverage of staff responding unpaid to emergency calls. There was a continuous stream of PR initiatives so that the government was always on the back foot. Roger was made to have a new sleek haircut and was always dressed in a business suit.

Roger rarely, if ever, used the argot of the union movement. It was never a question of "our members" - which in the public's mind might smack of a sectional interest - It was always "Britain's ambulance men and women". It seemed to work. "They weren't trade unionists first, they were first and foremost ambulance workers – the people who come to your aid at times of crisis in your life.

"One of the big problems with industrial disputes is that union officials seem to be arguing for a particular group of workers at the expense of everyone else, particularly in the public sector. We wanted to make sure we aligned ambulance crews with the public. People want a high quality ambulance service and we were determined to show that we wanted the same."

The techniques employed were not entirely new to the labour movement. In the rail dispute during the summer of 1989, Jimmy Knapp, general secretary of the National Union of Railwaymen, had successfully projected himself as the commuters' friend.

But the union campaign during the ambulance dispute achieved at an unprecedented level of sophistication. While it can be far more difficult to win public sympathy for other groups of workers, the approach of the Famous Five has provided the yardstick by which other union PR strategies have since been judged.

By contrast the government's efforts were leaden-footed, misconceived and ineffective. A "dirty tricks" campaign by ministers in late November back-fired spectacularly. Kenneth Clarke, for instance, told the Commons that the Bristol Road ambulance station in Birmingham failed to accept 999 calls for a 48-hour period. He said that one crew had refused to attend an accident in which a man lost a foot. The Birmingham Post found out that during the period in question the Bristol Road station had dealt with 50 emergency calls. The man with the severed foot turned out to be a woman who subsequently received seven stitches in a cut. A government advertising campaign aimed at shifting opinion had no discernible impact.

In October the Government tried another tack. Clarke announced that the staff side of the Whitley Council was insufficiently representative and that he intended to establish negotiating machinery in parallel with it. This body would incorporate the Association of Professional Ambulance Personnel (APAP) a non-TUC organisation set up in the wake of the 1980 health dispute. This "union" failed to win any traction from its new status – either with members of the TUC unions or the public. Even its own members were unimpressed by its leadership and rejected a repackaged nine per cent offer. Eventually APAP members voted by 6 to 1 to accept the proposals endorsed by the TUC unions.

The nine per cent offer, which emerged in negotiations in mid-November, illustrated the government's belated acknowledgment that it was losing the presentational battle. The offer of 6.5 per cent over a year was turned into 9 per cent over 18 months. It did not take a mathematician to work out that it was essentially the same. But thence forward Clarke routinely referred to "the nine per cent offer", failing to point out that it was to be spread over a year and a half.

Meanwhile at the House of Commons Bob Abberley was quietly beavering away, targeting Tory MPs who might be persuaded to break ranks with the Government. Bob managed for instance, to elicit support from the Conservative MPs Richard Holt, Jerry Hayes and Peter Temple-Morris, who nearly ten years later joined the Labour Party. It was all part of the strategy to erode the Government's political base. At one stage the unions decided to employ a lobbying company run by Conservatives – a ploy never before tried by a union in dispute – which gave Roger and his colleagues much greater access to the corridors of power.

The denouement came in the small hours of 23 February 1990. Both sides were closeted at a brutally ugly 60s building at the Elephant and Castle in south London which was the Department of Health's headquarters at the time.

Talks went on throughout the night with NHS chief executive Duncan Nichol calling for occasional adjournments. Roger is convinced that Nichol was leaving the talks to give progress reports to the Secretary of State and to seek his approval for any tinkering with the new offer. Ostensibly the union negotiating team was dealing with Nichol, but he had no leeway whatsoever. There is no doubt that everything had to be run past Clarke or his lieutenants.

As the hours went by, a room set aside for journalists – most of whom were equipped with the new brick-sized "portable phones" - became increasingly crowded. A meal was sent over for the union negotiators by canteen workers at the nearby St Thomas's Hospital. Ever-conscious of PR, some of the food was sent to the waiting television crews, radio reporters and newspaper journalists. Management had to make their own arrangements.

A complicated two year deal was finally thrashed out in the early hours of 23 February and ambulance staff accepted the package by four to one on March 15. The unions calculated that they had achieved a pay rise of 17.6 per cent on basic rates over two years rising to 24.6 per cent for qualified staff. The government however claimed the increase in the wage bill was only 13.3 per cent.
The main points of the settlement were as follows:
(a) A lump sum covering the period April 1989 - 1 March 1990
(b) A 9 per cent consolidated increase from 1 March 1990 to 30 September 1990
(c) A further increase of 7.9 per cent from 1 October to 30 March 1991
(d) Allowances in the range of £150-£500 a year for staff with various paramedic skills
(e) Local flexibility to give a target increase of no more than 2 per cent from 1 October 1990 on condition the money was found through savings

The government refused to countenance a pay mechanism, but agreed to establish a frame of reference for future pay negotiations by taking into account the following factors:

(1) Relevant pay movements in the health service
(2) Internal pay differentials
(3) Affordability
(4) The need to develop local flexibility within a national framework to address recruitment and retention problems and the need to solve career and pay structure problems.*

Following the marathon talks, Roger said in TV and radio interviews that the deal had driven a "coach and horses" through the Government's pay policy – a controversial comment at the time.

Most observers believed that the settlement was an advance, in the sense that it gave ambulance workers a deal spread over a longer period. But the Government had successfully resisted a pay mechanism and there were a number of ifs, buts and maybes in the detail.
Roger believes that the real advance was in the recognition that the skills of ambulance staff needed to be fostered and recognised.

"I don't regret the 'coach and horses' quote. I think we had a very good deal and I wanted to put it in sharp terms. May be it was the right thing to say, may be it wasn't. It is clear that the dispute did stop the privatisation being planned and even the Tories were forced to put money into training. You have to remember that only a minority of ambulance crews had training as paramedics before the dispute. In the 70s I remember many ambulance stations organised bring and buy sales to pay for defibrillators and intubators for their vehicles. Staff in some areas would have to go on courses in their own time to become paramedics. Ken Clarke had refused to train or equip crews properly and the BMA also opposed it. Essentially they saw ambulance crews as a 'scoop and drive' service – picking up accident victims and getting them to hospital as soon as possible."

A Sheffield University study commissioned some time before the conflict showed that on a conservative estimate 5,000 lives a year would be saved if half the workforce were trained as paramedics. "During the dispute Ken Clarke jumped on the paramedic bandwagon and called for proper training, conveniently forgetting what he'd previously said."

So who won? "It was a draw, but it turned into a huge victory down the line. The service was professionalized - the government was shamed into providing training - and the rates now paid to ambulance crews are very good. And all that came about because of the dispute.
"It also showed that unions can come together and can put a case to their employer, to the Government and to the people which makes sense. When workers don't do that they often lose. Low-paid workers especially have a hard time and they deserve trade unions which win for them and which don't lead them to successive defeats."Our claim was not extortionate and we said all along that we were prepared to go to arbitration. That rational approach to industrial relations, coupled with the kind of responsible behaviour shown by the ambulance crews, is the sort of trade unionism that can win."

Barrie Clement is former Labour Editor and Transport Editor of The Independent

* British Journal of Industrial Relations, March 1992. "Third among Equals: An Analysis of the 1989 Ambulance Dispute" by NUPE research officers Allan Kerr and Sanjit Sachdev.

Chapter 1: A weak bridge

The bridge across the river feeder to the ambulance station has always been weak, only allowing one vehicle in either direction at any one time. Over the years, it strained under the weight of the increasingly heavier ambulances that crossed its short span with a frequency that no-one building it could ever have anticipated. The commitment to 'go on a bluey' was made by the time the ambulance front wheels touched the bridge section with blue lights flashing and horns blaring to warn the traffic out on to North Road to slow down.

North Road is the busiest arterial road into and out of the centre of Cardiff. By 9.30 any weekday morning it had carried thousands of vehicles from the valleys to the North of the city and had digested the feed of the many suburbs all battling for daily spaces so workers could perform their function during office hours, blissfully unaware that the city had been busy for three or four hours with factory car parks already full. The average car in 1989 would not have had airbags, self tensioning seat belts, disc brakes on all four wheels, side impact protection and most of the "passive" and "active" safety that seems standard twenty years on. The wearing of rear seat belts had only been compulsory for a few years and many passengers just did not wear them, even in the front seats. You can imagine that the consequences of a road traffic accident (now officially called "collision") would be far more serious for the occupants then than now.

No one could have envisaged that by the end of the year the sound of sirens from the ambulances speeding up the drive from Blackweir Ambulance Station in Cardiff would be replaced by the cacophony of sound at the "top of the drive" from motorists slowing down to beep their horns in support of the locked out workers stood at the entrance to the station. With placards waving and buckets held aloft for lorry drivers to throw coins in or held at window level when the hand indicated there was a financial contribution to the fund coming, traffic slowed down to demonstrate support for the Ambulance Workers - a phrase recently coined and latched on to by the public.

The pay deal struck in April 1986 had been voted for by all UK ambulance staff who were informed by bulletin that their wish to be considered "more professional", lose their ancillary status and move towards a professional and technical status was in their hands. The changes were glaring: a move from weekly to monthly pay; the end of clocking in (nurses didn't clock in at the hospital); an all-in salary with no separate unsocial hours payments (as in the past); overtime payments at the normal single rate; a change in the way annual leave was administered from retrospective to current; and a rise in pay - which on the surface looked like a better deal for staff. These changes were close to something everyone had been striving for in the dozen years since the NHS took complete control of the service. The old image of ambulance staff as the local council ex-bus driver with a first aid certificate from St John's Ambulance Brigade was gone forever.

It was the three years of erosion of the pay elements of the deal coupled with the realisation that we had lost more than we gained, especially the enhancements that we had become used to, that started the build up of tension. This led to the six month National Ambulance Dispute from October 1989 till March 1990. The foundations of the April 1986 deal were weaker than the bridge at Blackweir Ambulance Station and led directly to the 1989 dispute.

The focus of the pay claim with Prime Minister Mrs Thatcher's team of negotiators (including Kenneth Clarke and Ann Widdecombe) was the comparison and demand for parity with a fifth year fire fighter. For the entire three year period of the 1986/89 bridge these fire fighters were earning more than both emergency ambulance staff and the more highly qualified paramedics in every part of the UK.

There was a tension building that no-one predicted would lead to the events of late 1989 - events that would determine and inform not only everything that has happened to me since, but to the Service itself which would change beyond recognition forever from that point.

Twenty years has a certain familiar ring to it: "It was twenty years ago today, Sgt. Pepper taught the band to play" sang Paul on the Beatles' Sgt .Pepper album in 1967 and I have a twenty year cycle theory that applies to my job as a Paramedic and the events that were central to the 1989/90 dispute. In 1948 when the NHS was set up with the rest of the Welfare State, Aneurin Bevan, Minister for Health in the post war government declared that "the verb is more important than the noun". The vision and determination he demonstrated in a mammoth achievement makes me so proud to have had the thinnest thread of a connection to him 60 years later. But however deeply I search, it is very hard for me to align the post-war Ambulance Service to the NHS until the 1960s. It was then that the home of the Ambulance Service was identified as the NHS and not the local councils. They received funding to run Ambulance Services in both rural and urban areas in a patchwork quilt affair until the ambulance service was eventually brought within the NHS in 1974.In 1966, in a report for the Minister for Health, the Working Party on Ambulance Training and Equipment, chaired by Doctor Millar, made the link between ambulance training and the equipment used. The report was ultimately adopted by the UK Government as the basis for the course and certificate that defined "qualified" ambulance staff. Also in 1966, whilst Consultant Physician at Belfast's Royal Victoria hospital, Doctor Frank Pantridge invented the portable defibrillator using car batteries and weighing in at 70 kg. In 1969, utilising these "portable defibs" inside a vehicle (that's what we call an Ambulance) he piloted a trial in Belfast to put cardiac doctors on ambulances to go into the community that had the worst rates of coronary illness, disease and survival rates from heart attack in the whole of the UK. The trial proved very successful with the breakthrough that doctors could train ambulance staff to be their "hands and eyes" in the community if they followed a protocol the doctors themselves trained them in.

Doctor John Michael Criley in Los Angeles wasted no time in 1969 and has the first recognised Paramedic Programme to his name in which he trained the firefighters of the county. The word "Paramedic" was used in his report for the first time outside a military context (think of TV series M*A*S*H).

Within a few years the principles set out by Doctor Criley had travelled across the rest of the USA which widely adopted the Paramedic principle. In the USA a few years earlier in 1966 saw the publication of **Accidental Death and Disability: The Neglected Disease of Modern Society,** also referred to as the White Paper. This acknowledged that soldiers and victims of trauma in the Vietnam War stood a better chance of survival than road accident casualties back home because of the intensive training of the "medics". By 1972 the public heard the word "Paramedic" on the television in a series called "Emergency". It would take another ten years, well into the mid 1980s, and still within the 20 year theory window, that the term Paramedic would be in common use in the UK with the introduction of the NHS model of practice (even though papers written by pioneers such as Douglas Chamberlain were published in the Lancet and BMJ as early as 1973).

Chapter 2: Half a tomato season

Me as new recruit 1985

The ambulance dispute took place in 1989 - just four years after the end of the miners' strike and the scars had hardly started to heal within the trade union movement. Without doubt the pit strike was the most significant dispute in post war Britain and, together with the legislation removing trade union rights and freedoms, was beginning to define Margaret Thatcher's Conservative government that had been in power for a decade. The dispute was personified by the NUM leader Arthur Scargill and the Coal Board Chairman Ian McGregor and was a fight for jobs. The press had a field day vilifying Scargill on a daily basis dragging up virtually every detail of his life, leaving McGregor relatively low profile.

But a lot happened to me before this. I first became a union member when I joined the civil service from school during Jim Callaghan's ill-fated government in the late 1970s.

I felt very strange that my mum and dad were so proud that I would be working in the Law Courts (it was actually called the Lord Chancellor's Department) and as my Dad put it had secured a "job for life" but within days of arriving I felt the industrial unrest brewing up elsewhere in the Civil Service. I eventually transferred from the County Court (divorces and summonses) to the Crown Court (juries and criminals) and sat a board to gain promotion and ended up in the default department of Companies House because of my perceived legal experience.

It was there that was to be called the 'winter of discontent' became a reality for me and we were "out" as often as we were in, the place virtually a closed shop (a phrase never heard since). It had struck me that although I had met some extremely interesting people in the Dept. Of Trade and Industry one or two in particular have remained life-long friends that I was not well cast in the role of civil servant and gained what knowledge and experience I needed very quickly and moved on.

The Army taking patients to hospital in Cardiff during the winter of discontent 1978/79

By 1981 jobs were becoming scarce for the first time since the war and unemployment was raging. I was quick to appreciate the benefits of working in the public sector and wanted something more fulfilling to me than a desk job, the lure of the hospital with its gothic facade must have been a subliminal influence when I wrote the letter to the head porter and the general manager enquiring about a potential vacancy. I mentioned that I had been a patient overnight the year before and was very impressed with the atmosphere of the place. They interviewed me I think more out of curiosity as the portering dept. was staffed more by ex-steelworkers and men in the twilight of their careers whilst there was full employment a couple of years earlier and I became at that time the youngest general porter. I made a decision to work in the NHS whilst being on the shortlist for a BBC job that to this day still interrupts my thoughts with the "What if?" questions that life can pose. But as I went beyond the shortlist to an actual job offer in 1982 as the Falklands War was just starting, with all the talk of potential conscription that was being muted, I felt I had taken the safest option.

As soon as I joined Cardiff Royal Infirmary I became a member of COHSE (the Confederation of Health Service Employees) in July 1982. Within the hospital I had plenty of opportunities to learn the lie of the land. I particularly enjoyed stints in theatres and the mortuary. I was often called to run from theatre to the blood bank when the operation was still ongoing to refresh supplies. I changed gases in intensive care knowing the patients lying there could never personally thank me and I helped road accident victims out of the ambulance when the crew radioed ahead of their arrival. I collected waste food in buckets and brought it out the side road where the pig farmer would collect it in his lorry and I walked grieving relatives down the long corridor to the morgue when they had to identify the bodies of loved ones.

Within a month of starting at the hospital, I was out on the gate in a strike that was supposed to be NHS wide but clearly had high profile hotspots. It was here that I learned the "theory" about emergency cover. Of course, nothing in the dispute must pose a risk to patients and there were many unions in the hospital including a couple of Royal Colleges. By the time the "emergency cover" was written up and applied to all the wards, theatres, clinics, labs and departments there seemed to be more staff in work on a day of action than on normal days, the only people actually on strike and losing money were the porters, domestics and catering staff who were the mainstay membership of the Confederation of Health Service Employees (COHSE) and the National Union of Public Employees (NUPE).

There seemed a very well orchestrated "organisation" locally that ensured this ward and that unit was always covered and that in the case of the porters "the front desk" that decided which requests for jobs were to be allocated to porters on emergency cover and which jobs would have to be done by someone else always had to be covered . That seemed a bit futile to me because the whole of the portering "pool" were out on the front and side gates picketing the hospital, even though there were at least half a dozen other entrances to the hospital through the labs, pathology or nursing quarters that weren't being picketed and staff could make their daily entrance through those portals to undertake their "emergency cover". The public didn't really realise much of a difference in the service provided and very little was done publicly to garner support which could never therefore be measured. It just looked like a few militants from the great unwashed were standing around the entrances protesting. A little bit of research on my Honda C90 scooter around the other hospital sites in the city brought forth a very graphic image that apart from a few posters at their gates, our hospital was the only one in the health authority flying the flag with a constant human shield of ancillary staff including newly appointed me holding firm on at least an 18 hour a day vigil outside. The whole issue came to a head when a few weeks into the 1982 NHS pay dispute when there were proposals to share the pay from emergency cover amongst the strikers just receiving strike pay. The action was very short lived and bitterly divided loyalties staff had to each other in the hospital in the aftermath although there has never been an NHS wide strike or dispute since 1982 that affected the whole workforce or country.

Whilst walking the corridors at night I would read the plaques outside wards which owed their name either to the benevolence of a single person or the collective of a whole colliery or a trade union whose predecessors helped build the place. I learned about the battle of Mametz Wood in the First World War and soldiers coming back and needing medical assistance in the ward that was later named after the battle. I learnt that after 100 years of service the hospital became part of the NHS in July 1948. I knew I had become part of a family in work. The membership of the union meant to me that I could play an active role within the family. However it didn't take that long for me to extend right up to the boundaries of responsibility within the whole portering role. A couple of years in, my feet were beginning to itch and I was conscious that Infirmary life was a stepping stone to something else which would at least be better paid.

My daily contact with ambulance crews and their work was based mostly around me being asked to assist in Casualty when a serious case was about to arrive at the dedicated Ambulance entrance and then help the crew take the patient to the "crash" room where the team of Doctors and nurses would be waiting. The Radiographer and I were often asked to stay behind in case we were needed. For me that usually meant a run to the blood bank or trolley dash to theatre. It took me a while to realise they didn't just deal with crashes in the room but anything life threatening.

Quite often during day shifts I would go with the crew down to the ambulance liaison office in fracture clinic to hear the story of how the accident occurred and the tales of what they found when on scene. The liaison officer was a portly chap called George Sylvester who, once the crew were sent on their way, would always ask me to stay behind and get the cuppas and Chelsea buns from the WRVS because he couldn't leave the phone in case another emergency was coming in. During these chats, in which George told me stories about cases he attended 20 years previously in the early 1960s when he was on the road, we built up quite a rapport. He was interested in my family background and told me in great detail of how his family in Russia fled the Nazis and ended up in Wales when he was a little boy. He had a great accent mixing Welsh slang with a Russian dialect - something I identified with closely as my mother's Italian dialect informs her Welsh phrasing. It was George who persuaded me that it might be worth me applying for a job in the Ambulance Service and when there were vacancies he let me know and as it was to be an inter-NHS transfer then he would help oil the wheels of the application and offered to be my reference. Sadly, within a few months of the application process going through and my successful transfer, George fell ill and after a year of ill-health retirement he passed away and we hadn't managed many of those chats and cuppas with me in the role of the crew and him unable to leave the phone.

My interview was with the Chief Ambulance Officer, Keith Goodall and the Deputy Chief, Dave Lyden, two proud Scousers who noted my love of music on the application form and spent most of the interview discussing the Beatles and Kate Bush. George must have put in a good word because the kind of questions I was expecting didn't come up and there was quite an emphasis on the fact that my mother was an Italian and they wanted as rich and diverse a service as possible (there is a big Italian community in Cardiff but as the image of great diet and old age testifies there isn't a large proportion of Italian 999 calls). They did say they were looking for the new breed of staff willing to train as "Paramedics", a word that was brand new, as the BBC hospital drama Casualty was just about to hit the screens within a year. This changed everything that the public had previously thought and perceived about the role. Up until then the image was like the Ambulance Drivers portrayed in the Carry On Doctor films .

So I started in the Ambulance Service in 1985. For the first couple of years my job was that of outpatient crew. We would take day cases to hospital clinics and centres for routine pre-arranged appointments and undertake inter hospital transfers sometimes going far afield with patients and medical escorts on away jobs to London, Manchester, Plymouth or Birmingham but mostly staying locally. The ambulance station was home to both the emergency crews (the same ones I had got to know from the hospital) and the unqualified staff who wore the same uniform, drove similar vehicles or hand me down emergency vehicles but were differentiated by a small sewn on cloth badge worn proudly on the left arm of the NATO jumper of the qualified staff. A laurel wreath insignia indicated the wearer had passed the emergency course set out by Doctor Millar in his 1966 report on training.

The other badge allowed to be worn was of their union and in those days there was a 70/30 split between NUPE and the General and Municipal Workers (GMBWU, later just the GMB). I felt a bit isolated as I had risen to the auspicious rank of branch auditor at the Infirmary but found that there was no COHSE branch in the local Ambulance stations and only one member of COHSE in all the region (I found out later that he had been the previous NUPE branch secretary but after a row locally was ousted from NUPE and needed to find a home with some union but had vowed never to join GMB). I joined NUPE as I had nearly joined the branch in the hospital. I was also friends with a couple of the branch people who I had met in the porters' room when support was building amongst health unions for the miners in 1984 at the beginning of the strike. The porters' room was an unofficial place for any passing miners to be made welcome with a coffee and chat, the Infirmary mostly built or added on to by the benevolence and camaraderie of the miners themselves at the beginning of the century.

Like everyone entering the Service I was initially employed transporting patients to their routine outpatient appointments to hospital. Some of the elderly and mentally ill patients regularly travelled to the same day unit - in some cases every day of the week. These journeys were arranged so we picked up six or eight patients, one after the other and the city and county were carved up into zones. We called these regular runs "zone runs" and they were the mainstay of my first couple of years. In between zone runs we would be sent to the outpatient department at the main hospitals where in the Ambulance Liaison Office the Officer would assign return journeys back home from the various clinics. The geography of zones bore no relation to the miles apart these patients sometimes lived and we would often be late for our afternoon pick-ups at the day unit.

I had to wait my turn to qualify to go on emergencies and did my time on outpatients work, until the day I would be sent on the residential course in one of the national training schools in Keighley, Banstead or Chippenham. Of course, because I was not on emergencies or qualified in 1986, the emergency crews rarely talked to me beyond politeness, especially at the hospital. My position in the Service was slightly above rookie status because I had known most of the crews from my previous four years at the hospital. I still hadn't completed a full tomato picking season in some people's eyes. I got into the habit of making tea for them just as they pulled down the drive to the station and over the bridge "at the point of need" whenever I was on the station.

Within a few months in the Ambulance Service I had been elected a steward by my colleagues and went on my first course run by the local Further Education college. It was at this time that the details of the upcoming pay deal were becoming known and as a newly qualified steward with hospital experience I was helping inform the debate at the NUPE branch meetings. There was clearly some resistance from older staff who had been in the comfort zone of having the same terms and conditions for years, determined by what was called the Ambulance Whitley Council - a joint union-management body which met in Leeds every year and worked out the pay rise for all staff (very little else was up for negotiation).

I found out that there was a Whitley Council for all workers in the NHS, nurses, ancillary admin and clerical but that doctors and dentists had their pay decided in a very different way, through a pay review body. Once Christmas 1985 was out of the way we were asked by the unions to vote to accept or reject the pay deal for the following April. There was not too much time for anyone to get into the details or small print but it was clear that there were some radical changes on the table following negotiations that most of us did not even know were taking place.

The most pressing change was the move from being paid weekly to being paid monthly direct into bank accounts. We were given very little option about how we would move from weekly pay to the first monthly pay and how we would manage the fallow weeks when the system would go from retrospective to prospective in calculating leave entitlements. There was also an all-in salary proposed that would pay overtime at plain rate instead of time and a half and eliminate separate unsocial hours payments or night allowances as they were known. The sweeteners in this deal were a pay rise to bring an emergency ambulance person in line with (parity they called it) a fifth year fire fighter (who earned more) and an end to the practice of clocking on and off at the start and end of shifts which would be in recognition of the more professional status it seems we were seeking and nationally was being acknowledged. Being a newish steward meant I did not have many cases to deal with and very little to cut my teeth on, so putting up posters and engaging in workplace conversations on the pros and cons of the deal became the mainstay of my NUPE responsibilities in between taking "Nana" to hospital.

To me it was very clear that most members had been hypnotised with what they had worked out with a calculator in the deal rather than thinking about anything beyond the pay. Nurses were not the group that staff associated with as comparators at that time and the Fire Service had an affinity with most crews on the ground. Everyone in work knew that they earned more and shared the same 'phone number' so the parity with a fifth year fire fighter was a real achievement. We looked to fire fighters rather than nurses, even though we worked side by side with them. If we had aligned closer with the nurses, we would have seen that they did not get paid weekly, did not have to clock in but did not cash in all of their entitlements hard earned over 40 years in a weird one off pay deal like we were even contemplating.

The die had been cast by the time of the ballot. The overwhelming view was that to achieve a pay rise during Thatcher's second term was an achievement, the peripheral elements of the deal were barely considered as important. I remember speaking with a member of qualified staff who had worked at the station since the early 1960s, and he told me he was voting for the deal because he remembered the last big rise was when the staff moved from the Local Authority control to NHS control in 1974. Before that the only pay rise was if someone got themselves a recognised first aid certificate. Things had come a long way.

To alleviate fears of "going over" to monthly pay the principal union reps had a series of negotiations with the Chief and a couple of the hospital finance people to cushion the fallow weeks with what ended up an interest free loan. These interest free loan talks locally were emphasised at meetings. The national negotiations increasingly referred to salary structure proposals, but most just saw it as this year's settlement to be voted on. The small print of the details faded into obscurity with most staff needing to know how they were to make the move to monthly pay before they cast their votes.

During these early months of 1986 like many other staff I talked the issues over at home with my girlfriend, Sonia. We had lived together since before I had worked at the Infirmary and we had bought our first house about four years before and it had been quite a stretch financially. Sonia had been working in the NHS as a dental nurse since school and was acutely aware of the Whitley scales and most of the issues resulting from the ambulance proposals. She was paid monthly which helped our domestic financial arrangements. There was no pressure for me to sign the deal.

I was clearly in the minority warning people to think more about what they were giving up than what would be gained. I knew the job was going to shed the ancillary image it had, including the clocking in and weekly pay soon, as I with a few dozen others had been told that we were the new wave of ambulance staff, soon to be the new paramedics, trailblazing the future with our professionalism.

I found out that every subsequent intake had been told the same thing and these words had become a bit hollow with some staff believing that they were in some way a new standard, a new vanguard and there were tensions brewing based on the elitism that some felt was ruining the collective strength.

The Ambulance Service, not just in Wales but all over the UK, was nigh on 100% unionised (now described as maximum density). The run down rest rooms at most ambulance stations had lockers bearing old stickers on the doors from previous unsuccessful pay claims going back over 20 years. These campaigns centred on pay only (either in percentage or flat rate increases demanded) and this was the first time terms and conditions appeared in the small print of the deal. The personalities and negotiators belonging to the union were pretty well unknown to us as members at this crucial stage and the NUPE offices at Grand Depot Road in London did not have a telephone helpline or Ambulance desk awaiting queries from members, so as activists locally we just had each other to rely on and the occasional letter from UNION HQ.

There didn't seem to be any network to find out what was happening in other branches or services. Training to be qualified put you on a course with 40 or so other students - in my case mostly from the south of England - and there was a certain amount of communication amongst us but it was limited. So the union letters of communication every year became more crucial and on arrival they were placed on the station in a special locked cabinet backed with a notice board for which only very senior stewards had a key. No letters were as crucial as the ones arriving in autumn 1989.

Chapter 3: It's not a strike - it's a dispute

We were not going to end up on strike - that's what everyone was saying. During the local meetings accompanying the national payround in 1989, tension was running high and we all had to work out whether there was an appetite for any action to back up our claim. Most staff felt that something big was brewing. It was about pay. It was all about pay. Since the 1986 deal, pay had fallen back year on year till we, as qualified staff, were well behind the average fifth year fire fighter - the recognised realistic comparator (no–one even mentioned parity with the police who had been given a substantial rise following the miners' strike some four years earlier). Now we had slipped behind again to become the lowest paid emergency service, albeit the busiest one.

Our meetings were attended usually by just a few members and were more a source of information than involvement prior to that autumn. Stalwarts of previous battles attended religiously and the ramshackle old geriatric ward that had been closed down by the hospital some years before but still had its heating left on was the usual venue and had an air of "Dad's Army" about the proceedings. Nothing was too formal. It was mostly over within the hour and very rarely continued in the pub afterwards. Colleagues said their bit and went home. As a relatively new steward I was always trying to liven things up and pose suggestions that might help with the negotiations with the Chief - that as a rookie I was always excluded from.

The first of the letters from the Joint Unions picked up on a feeling of unrest in the country but was never read out at a meeting. It was decided that the four main unions that had anything to do with the Ambulance Service - NUPE, GMB, COHSE and the National and Local Government Officers Association (NALGO, which later formed UNISON with NUPE and COHSE) - would pool resources and strategy in the handling and management of the pay negotiations that had seriously faltered and were in stalemate. The Transport and General Workers' Union (TGWU) was a partner but prior to the dispute we did not have one person in membership even though quite a few of the NUPE members used to work for the "Corporation" or Council on the buses.

An almighty row broke out at a joint branch meeting that took place around the time of the first letter. There were suggestions that the outpatient crews were to be first in line and that the first step in the action was linked to staff not undertaking outpatient work. There was not enough clarity about what this actually meant and during the meeting a key vote was suspended with outpatient crews present not at all happy that they alone should shoulder the burden of the action and the emergency crews carry on with "emergency cover".

The second letter that arrived indicated that we should get ready as emergency crews to stop undertaking the non-emergency side of the job, that is, the qualified staff assisting the outpatient crews in fulfilling the contracts with the local Health Authority for the zone run patients as well as the odd journey into a local clinic. This provided the clarity that had blighted the earlier joint branch meeting. The Service determined that these were non-emergency core duties. Most weekdays and every weekend 999 qualified staff would leave the station in their emergency wagon with the armrests pulled down from the back of each trolley cot and pick up as many as eight Nanas or Gramps with mostly mild symptoms of mental illness from various suburbs and transport them to the Day Unit at the hospital (in our case called the Royal Hamadryad) to what I used to think was unkindly labelled the Psycho Geriatric ward where they had their appointments. When first qualified I thought it seemed bizarre that I would be trained up residentially for months to come back and daily be expected to go out to the same Nanas I picked up for the previous three years when I was unqualified. I knew that part of the appeal for the emergency boys would be that they were guaranteed a cooked breakfast on completion of the run and there would always be a scramble on station to get to the Hamadryad as the breakfast was legendary. Little did we know that the practice of qualified staff routinely sent on pre-arranged zone runs for non-emergencies was commonplace across all Services.

In the letter to branches, the joint unions asked that we give notice to our Service of our intention to suspend that practice by the end of October and that 999 crews should and would only do 999 calls. As a steward I received a copy of this letter and was waiting patiently for the meeting to be called to hear the members' views and vote on the matter. After all it was a strategy that was designed to unify the country in its claim that ambulance staff were underpaid and was symbolic that it ticked the old "emergency cover" box that we had to abide by.

The newspapers had already been reporting the tensions building with headlines such as "Mercy Crews Wait Patiently" on the 16th October 1989 and the following day "Ambulancemen Plan 3 Day Fast", Roger Poole from NUPE stating that five or six staff were fasting at the Department of Health's Whitehall offices and two or three would be at each of the 14 Regional Health Authority Buildings. Needless to say we had a great laugh deciding which two or three of our staff should fast on the steps of the Temple of Peace, the old War Office building given over to the NHS in 1948. Perhaps not surprisingly, the fasting stunt did not eventually materialise in my city and county.

Various reasons seemed to hold up the members meeting on the real matter of "just" providing emergency work and foregoing the routine outpatient work and I remember using the letter to bolster interest in the forthcoming meeting. I had the hardest time persuading a pair of old timers on the station called George and Wally who were inseparable and always found in the canteen of the Geriatric hospital. However George was the only COHSE steward and the only COHSE member in the whole county service so he had already had a copy of the letter signed by Bob Abberley of his union and Donna Covey from the GMB so he knew it would not be long before NUPE called a meeting.

I remember the meeting well. Roger and Bob the NUPE branch officers (who confusingly shared the same first names as two of the national negotiators) went with Vyv and the other Roger from GMB to see the Chief to tell him ahead of the meeting that we were on a plan of action that would include not taking outpatients to the day units. This was a crossroads that would involve all members taking action, the qualified staff a partial action and the outpatient crews effectively with no role left for them at work if it went ahead. At what was the first of the big dispute meetings, the members sat and listened patiently to the response from the Chief and how disappointed he was in all of us for even contemplating taking action such as this. However the mood of the members was to follow this course of action and, following a unanimous vote, it was decided to give notice to suspend non-emergency work. The four local union officials were to tell management the following day. However, as we walked downstairs that night into the lobby of the station after the meeting finished, the Chief and his assistant were stood at the bottom of the stairs. He had a good look at everyone and had the appearance of the headmaster welcoming back the losing team to the school.

It didn't take very long for a formal response to be received and it was so significant that it warranted an emergency meeting just to read it out. Our Chief was a member of the Association of Chief Ambulance Officers, an invitation-only organisation of Chief Ambulance Officers with membership fees funded from taxpayers' money. This obviously came out of the budget for patients and the organisation was not accountable to anyone and was not formally part of the NHS. The year before an "offer" was made to any member of staff who wanted to become an "associate member" of this organisation to apply to the Assistant Chief for details and I knew one member of staff who successfully joined and one whose application was politely declined. There was no appeal if your membership was turned down as this exclusive club was beginning to become an old boys' network. They felt threatened as by the actions of the Trade Unions who were making demands of the Department of Health regarding Ambulance pay, so they started to network and as they all knew each other so well (they had annual dinners, presentation evenings and such like) they were sharing information or tactics initially much more effectively than the Unions. They hatched a plan which would prevaricate and provoke the situation to a point from which it would be extremely difficult to return.

The local paper, Western Mail was based a mile from the station and had sent a reporter, of course. Whilst we were upstairs deliberating he was downstairs in the same lobby as the Chief who was briefing him.

The story in the paper the next morning read “Patients Refused Lift Home”. “From midnight last night South Glamorgan crews are refusing to take patients home after treatment.” Roger Wimbush of NUPE said “We would be prepared to escalate our action further”. Andrew Dobbinson from GMB further explained “we will not be diverted except for cases of Dialysis, Cancer Care or the terminally ill”. The same article went on to state that 71 stations in London were closed, their Chief Officer Tom Crosby said “It’s Absolutely Disastrous”.

The meeting to hear our Chief’s response was more tense than the first meeting where the decision was taken to suspend Emergency crews from doing routine outpatient journeys. At least he had the courtesy to formalise his response to the negotiators rather than go to the press. We had debated to death the figures that constituted the 6.5% pay offer back in the summer. At that time some people were surprised that we had refused the offer that initially the union recommended we accept. So at this meeting we moved swiftly to discussing the ongoing management of the dispute.

One person had the Chief’s letter in his hand and when he read it the reaction in the room was palpable. The Chief had accepted our proposal and determined that outpatient work took up about 30% of our duties and if we were to suspend this routine function and concentrate on emergencies only he would ensure that our pay was cut by 30% accordingly. There was a real difficulty to try and keep any sort of order at the meeting and half an hour of mayhem followed this statement.

Many of the staff, including branch officials, were anxious, some scared of losing the 30%, with many stating that they would be unable to pay their mortgages and some others loudly stating that it was too big a sacrifice for a pay rise that had been previously recommended during the summer and refused by us. Some qualified staff even suggested that their unqualified colleagues shoulder the burden of pay cuts and leave it at that. This was the basis of the row at the branch meeting. The outpatient crews were to lose 100% of their wages to the qualified emergency crews 30%. The press were waiting outside the door and although nobody seemed in the mood for speeches, I spoke about the fact that this was going to play out publicly and that we had already received verbal support from relatives of patients who were well aware that we were on a pay campaign and the government was determined that we were not going to receive more.

I suggested that we would have no option but to get out collecting contributions from the public. I felt that as soon as the press reported that we were having a 30% pay cut whilst providing a 100% emergency service, there would be more than sympathy, there would be anger. I was told in no uncertain terms that we would be wasting our time, no one would give, and warned that the unions' funds could be seized as there had been recent legislation to that effect. Luckily, enough members agreed with me and there was no shortage of volunteers - especially from the ranks of the outpatient crews - to come into the city centre on Saturday to put the public's charity to the test. We had to show some form of united front and work out amongst ourselves who should say what, on behalf of the majority of the members who voted to take the action and be the spokesperson and inform the newspaper journalist waiting outside. Luckily the Chief's letter about the 30% pay cut wrote its own headline. As the next few weeks unfolded, the dynamic of not taking outpatients to hospital affected the staff's outlook on the seriousness of the action. Little did I know then that similar events were being played out in Ambulance Services all across the country.

Others in the medical profession knew what was happening because they often had to make alternative arrangements to get their routine patients in or on to the ward for treatment or therapy leaving us to do the 999 emergencies. We noticed on several occasions we would receive a 999 for a patient to go to an 'emergency' outpatient appointment. Virtually every non-emergency call they could get away with was being upgraded to a full blown emergency. Many of our control staff would pass these upgraded calls through, none the wiser to the ploy. Many headed this off at the pass but it must have been very difficult to tell a doctor: "Sorry, this doesn't sound like an emergency lights and horns job to me". This all just angered the crews who clearly were not being paid to do any outpatients appointments or zone runs, genuine or spurious ones. On a Sky News report in late October 1989 we learned that the green goddesses* those big wartime style fire engines built in Papworth hospital just after the war were already dusted down and commissioned to be deployed by the Army in London as contingency there as a result of the dispute locally beginning to bite.

The next letter from the various union headquarters just simply asked staff not to work overtime and was the first mention of an overtime ban. There had been 6 hours of peace talks at ACAS on the 25th October which were to continue and falter on the 26th October in what was described as a "wide gulf" between the parties.

On the 30th October the reports read "Ambulancemen To Step Up Dispute". There was to be far more than an overtime ban: detailing a tighter restriction of movement of staff from station to station, no changes in shift arrangements and no replacements when staff are on leave. The reports stated the Army were on standby. I knew from that moment on that things were never going to be the same again.

---

*green goddesses were Army vehicles in use at the end of the Second World War until about 1948. They were built in Papworth Hospital in an industrial offshoot of Papworth Industries, a legacy of the medical pioneer Sir Pendrill Charles Varrier Jones. I now live in the house he was born in. He founded the Hospital and Village Settlement on the principle that returning First World War soldiers and civilians who contracted Tuberculosis had better outcomes when their families were close by. They worked building the properties for their families to live in and later worked at the factory on the Papworth Hospital Estate in Cambridgeshire when they were well enough. In the 1970s and 1980s the same factory produced Ambulance bodies for the NHS fleet. As seen in the photograph the goddesses were multi - purpose fire or ambulance military vehicles occasionally deployed for contingency civilian use and were notoriously heavy and slow.

Chapter 4: the collecting

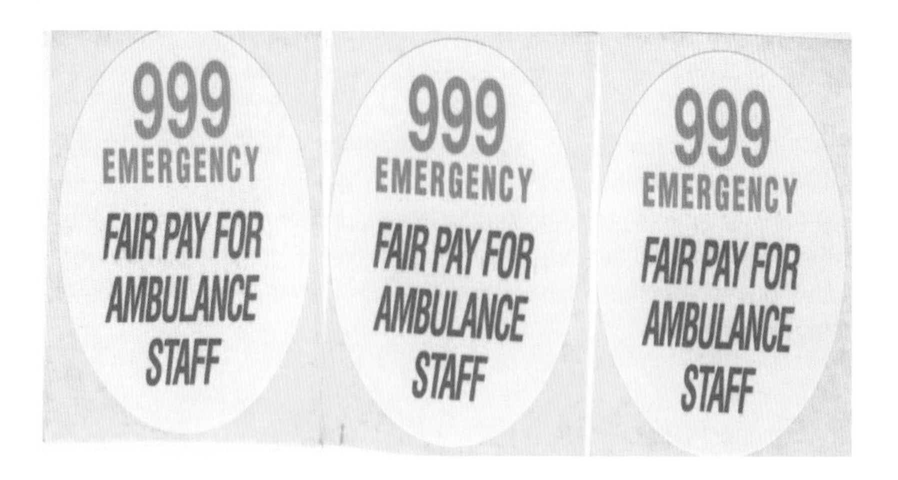

The hardware shop owner about half a mile from the Station couldn't believe his luck when we started buying the buckets, we pretty soon outstripped his stock and luckily they were predominantly bright red ones. We aimed for the first Saturday and about seven or eight of us were there including a couple of willing spouses. There were six actual staff in reflective jackets with placards and buckets, which still had the manufacturer's stickers on them next to the Union stickers. We chose three strategic spots to stand in twos. It was the end of October 1989: one bucket outside Marks and Spencer in the main shopping street, one outside the main railway station and one outside the indoor market entrance. There was a little bit of curiosity from passers by who must have faced an alarming image. Firstly it was a rare sight to see uniformed ambulance staff standing without a vehicle nearby, and nobody had seen ambulance staff collecting money in domestic plastic buckets before.

We wrongly assumed that most people would not have read or heard anything about our case as there had only been a story on Newsnight one late night about the pay issue. What started to happen was that we would loudly explain our case in a town cryer sort of manner. That was the downside for some of the volunteers who were collecting. Most people who know me realise that I have never needed a microphone in my life but it was funny in the first few minutes to hear my colleague get a bit tongue tied during the explanation bit leaving all the shouting to me.

We started about midday and – unbelievably - the story about the previous evening's meeting made the front page of South Wales Echo. "Ambulance Staff Face 30% Cut in Wages" was on every hoarding and paper stand all over the City Centre. Most of the public passing by the buckets were curious but by the time we borrowed the placard posters and a couple of copies of the paper we were gathering quite a crowd especially at the Marks and Spencer location. The manager of Marks came out to see what was happening and I recognised that he had been on my wagon a few weeks before when he had suffered a heart attack, so there was no objection from him. Similarly, the police would walk past the strange gathering of people listening to the story of the poor pay offer and the 30% cut, and make clear their sympathies. Considering we worked so closely with them locally, there were not going to be any scenes like in the miners' dispute involving ambulance staff. As the day went by, we noticed that the generosity of people was massive and was frequently accompanied by a story from the person after they had listened to the reasons for the collection. I often heard phrases like " I think you people are marvellous" and "what you people did for my Dad, husband, wife, brother etc" followed by at least a few pounds, but often a five or ten pound note into the bucket.

It dawned on me by about three o' clock in the afternoon that we had an enormous amount of money in our buckets and we decided to walk around to the others to see if it was just our pitch or whether they had also had a big collection. They had. There and then, on the spot we started to create the rules for collecting. Always in twos or threes; always count up afterwards; colleagues present to verify and to be dropped off and picked up at the end so no-one ran the risk of walking back to the station or union offices with buckets full of money. The total on the first day was a phenomenal £18,000 from just six collectors between twelve pm and five pm. It took over four hours to count it. We were still in the station close to midnight and those working on shift were shocked and it soon got to the branch officers that we had something big on our hands here.

As the person authorised by the branch to be the union official on the first day, I was effectively the instigator and had no idea whether I would sink or swim. No-one, none of us contemplated the combination of the newspaper headlines and the warmth and generosity of the public that day.

We really did underestimate how knowledgeable they were, mentioning their opinion of the Health Minister Kenneth Clarke as well as having a good understanding of the issue. I had a phone call the following day from the senior branch people instructing me to get down the bank on Monday morning to bank the lot - the location of the £18,000 was being kept secret. We had some basic books, but with Andrea from GMB and Graham also from NUPE, the three of us became the collection officers overnight. Following a piece or two of advice from Roger the branch secretary, I took a walk down to the bank on the corner near the hospital on Monday morning to ask for an appointment to open an account. No appointment was necessary and there was a little discussion about what to name the account. We did not want any of the unions' names in any way connected with it because there was a fear that the funds would be sequestrated (a word we had never heard until the Tories made new legislation with powers to seize funds from unions for any losses a strike caused). We turned up at the bank at lunchtime and proceeded to unload £18,000 and odd over the counter - mostly in coins. About halfway through the counting, the staff started to complain, not realising that this was collected in a few hours. Patience was wearing a bit thin in the bank as more and more staff had to count cash out of buckets. Of course we were strongly advised by them that this was to be a one off. We were to receive coin bags and sort out our own counting leaving the bank staff the job of weighing in the money on the scales.

We bought a ledger that day and jointly administered it, keeping it locked away from anyone and everyone, but to hand for us in one of the lockers. When we went to the next meeting, the severity of the pay cut was real and we had to recruit people to help with making up the shortfall in the wages. The whole idea was that there would be a payout of effectively shares in the collection, to be spread equally amongst all those who had received a cut, with a ceiling. The priority was the outpatient crews who had zero pay. There was an unwritten incentive to all crews to attend and collect to bolster the fund as we explained we might have to re-distribute everyone's wages if we didn't collect enough to pay everyone. So although it did not make 100% of the pay, there would be a couple of pounds available from the respective unions which was effectively strike pay (even though we were not actually on strike) that would make up the rest leaving a residual amount in the funds.

I had far less to do with the science and rationale of doling out the money than I did in the intricacies of collecting it but it wasn't long before I was roped in to do the pay packet for October 1989 and within a few weeks November's pay packet also.

Knowledge of the amount of "income" we raised was limited to the inner circle of about six of us and we had a pretty accurate picture of the amount to be paid out to make up the wages. How one simple thing can lead to 100 complications! We had the payslips collected directly from the payroll office at the hospital. From a previous meeting, we had "permission" or a mandate that as the NHS payslip would show how much was paid into the bank it would also show how much had been deducted and we could make up the shortfall with a combination of cheques drawn on the new account and a small amount of cash.

We had word that one paramedic was unhappy that we were going to open his payslip and that he intended to sue us if only he could find out which one of us it was and where we were. Pay day arrived and we were holed up in a small room in GMB's regional office under the supervision of their Full Time Officer for Health, Alan Rappel, when news came through that we were to be sued if we had opened the wage slip of a certain paramedic. Although the Chief Officer had briefly mentioned injunctions against us and had carried out his non-negotiable 30% pay cut, he did not add insult to injury by preventing us "topping" up the wages. He was also quite happy for the payslips to be sent to our secret location for the topped up pay-out.

I had already opened the payslip in question in the company of 3 other people when a phone message came through that I must not touch the particular payslip. But it was too late. We were prioritising the payslips of the outpatient crews (who were not getting any pay) to worry too much about what one paramedic said. We were using the payslips to help us balance our books and record how much was being paid out and to whom. Little did we realise that the person making all the fuss was not paying contributions to any union. That was his choice, but why didn't he say that to us instead of getting all out of proportion? We knew that he was afraid that he would have to shoulder the loss himself. Deductions for union contributions were deducted at source from the wages. As reps we thought we knew who were members and who were not but it was not a very sophisticated auditing system in place.

A small group of staff members joined the Association of Professional Ambulance Personnel (APAP) an organisation that had a link with Kenneth Clarke - albeit a loose one that appeared to commence in November 1989 when he granted them negotiating rights for the Ambulance Service. This was never going to amount to anything as they represented a tiny minority and could not get TUC recognition. Nevertheless, there were Government people overseen by Mr Clarke working to try to get them to the table. The APAP people all had the same mantra: "if there was only one union in the Ambulance Service we'd all join it". I found it bizarre as there were already five unions. Adding another non-recognised organisation with non-defined values to the equation at a time of real emergency was madness. When we had a look in the payslips (despite the threat of being sued for making up one particular person's wages in the same way as everyone else) we found there were about a dozen out of 500 staff who had dual membership, but only a handful who had severed their links to the Union. We didn't mind but we kept a watchful eye as the events were to unfold.

Chapter 5: public speaking and collections

During November and the beginning of December 1989, the buckets in the city centre were becoming a common sight. The original group of six or seven reps, including myself, were finding it very hard to maintain overall control of every collector; timings and supervision became very hard to monitor. We had no problem with the County crews because they all knew to go to the city centre offices of either COHSE, NUPE or GMB where full time officers would always verify and store the collection in the safe until one of us could get along to bank it. We even had the staff at the COHSE office going to the bank for us and got them a paying in book and it was a daily function of that particular office. However we had concerns that with Christmas shoppers starting early and finishing late we were sure that neighbouring counties who didn't have the reductions and cuts in pay were out collecting in "our" city centre. Once we had intelligence that crews that were not ours were out collecting we would always check that there was a deposit of the buckets, a count and a receipt from the union office but unfortunately that wasn't always the case.

Following the newspapers' interest in the genesis of the story as soon as developments were known we had the BBC and commercial radio stations running stories on their news bulletins, which did the collections no harm at all. I had become an official spokesperson for not just NUPE but all ambulance staff in the dispute. I was always very careful to note that we were not on strike, that we wanted to maintain 100% emergency service for the public but because we were not doing routine outpatient appointments we were having 30% of our salary cut. Very few journalists spent long on the reason we were in dispute in the first place although there was always a short introduction about the pay offer and the emphasis on the action and how it affected the public.

I was asked to go into the Red Dragon radio studios to be part of a phone-in style show as a guest. Every single caller said that we deserved more money in our wages and it was a scandal that we had to take action to achieve it but virtually everyone was horrified by the way we were being treated by the management. The BBC, with its commitment to 'balance' had management representatives invited as well as one of us, but the public reaction was always the same. We were receiving massive support with more to come.

There had been a dispute the previous year with the teachers who limped back to work after the bitterness and vitriol against the government had evaporated into the ether as more and more teachers returned to the classrooms. At the buckets we noticed lots of people would see us as a serious challenge to the government with many saying "remember the teachers last year, you stick it out and don't give up", followed by some comment about the government not caring. We seemed to have an almost symmetrical "I think you people are marvellous/do a wonderful job/looked after my relative" comments and contributions on the one hand and then the "don't let them beat you/stand firm and stand strong together" always coupled with a contribution on the other. We started a "hoot if you support us" placard line at the main arterial road by the main city centre station for a couple of weeks and we would often send a delegation with four or five placards around rush hour to another main route in or out of the city and always had the obligatory buckets.

Traffic would slow to a crawl allowing drivers to perfect the throw-coins-whilst-moving technique. A coach driver called Mike Williams would stop his valleys coach at rush hour holding up the traffic behind for us to jump aboard the coach and collect from his passengers. We started to have visitors turning up on the station, some people just wanted to give a donation whilst others would want to engage in a chat to be sure they had a full understanding of the facts from our perspective. Most everyone understood our wages had dropped behind the Fire Service and the nurses and we were offered 9% to be spread across 18 months which was the only variation of the 6.5% over one year.

Most people saw the issue as simple unfairness and economics although some were hoping that the unprecedented support for a trade dispute might have some resonance with their political ambitions. Amongst the individual visitors to the station, our placard line up or bucket collection points, it was clear that some were from organised groups, some of them politically affiliated and it was not long before I was asked to speak at a rally to be held at 10 a.m. one Saturday in the city centre. I didn't hesitate as Tony Benn was already booked to speak and I was the token "uniformed member". There had been a couple of these rallies already where the idea of a potential full blown ambulance dispute had been one of the topics. Considering we rarely started our collections before 11 a.m., we missed these meetings although a choir called simply "The Red Choir" had made a collection at the meeting the week before and decanted the money into one of our buckets.

The union that covered college lecturers was called NATFHE and at one of the local further education campuses they wanted a couple of us to turn up in uniform and give our side of what was being reported about our pay claim. I remember both myself and Kevin Dwyer who was an outpatient driver went to an event that they had advertised amongst the students. It was a bit daunting to speak in the canteen at lunchtime to all of the college lecturers and their students especially as only a year or so before I had been on my Stage 1 and 2 Stewards course at the same college.
The first of the city centre rallies I spoke at was a massive affair. I clambered onto the back of a flatbed trailer from an articulated lorry parked in Sophia Gardens and spoke at first nervously into the mike. Trying to ignore the vast numbers stood in front of me imagined I was in the canteen of the local college as I was a few days before. I remembered the students and lecturers' questions at the end and knew that I wouldn't be having questions here - it was to be more like a speech but I ended it by reciting those questions and answers to give as true a picture as I could. I had prepared no notes at all but there were a few of us with buckets so ended with "Support your local Ambulance Workers" a line I had heard Roger Poole from NUPE use on the TV. It was becoming clear that there was not a week elapsing without some form of escalation from one side or another. The management around the UK informed the unions that they were cancelling all training to try and shore up the emergency side of the service which was sporadic in some parts of the country.

On the 13th November 1989 in an article about the fall of the Berlin Wall four days earlier Ian Aitken wrote in the *Guardian*:

> If ministers are hoping that the events in Berlin will divert public attention from the ambulance dispute in the same way as they have overshadowed the Lawson crisis, I suspect they are in for a shock. There is genuine public anger over the Government's obduracy, not least among middle class voters in London constituencies which the Conservatives will have to hold if they are to beat Mr Kinnock's refurbished Labour Party. Quite why an intelligent and civilised man like Kenneth Clarke got himself into so damaging a dispute is difficult to understand. The only convincing explanation is that he has developed such a blind hatred for the health service unions that he can't think straight about them any more. The signs now are that the centrepiece of Mr Major's autumn statement will be a larger than expected increase in public spending, and that the allocation to Mr Clarke's Health Department will be the largest of them all. No doubt the idea is to lubricate the introduction of his NHS 'reforms' with cash. He could do a lot better for his government, as well as for the rest of us, if he spent a little of it on settling with the ambulance crews.

On 16th December 1989 the *Economist* reported:

> Christmas will soon bring its usual toll of road accidents and drunken brawls. But the people who normally clear up after the revellers - Britain's 20,000 ambulancemen - may well not be there this year. The ambulance dispute is 14 weeks old and seems no nearer a solution. The meeting on December 14th between the management of the National Health Service (NHS) and Roger Poole, the ambulance unions' chief negotiator, was little more than a ritual. On most substantial issues the two sides are as far apart as ever.

Chapter 6: Run your own ambulance service

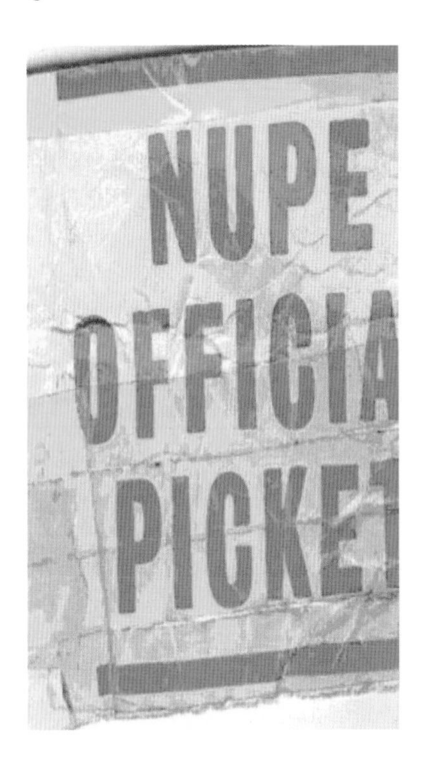

Most of the attendees at meetings were acutely aware that there was a difference in the agenda items that referred to local updates and events and the ones that had a national aspect. The letter read by the union negotiators following our pay cut needed to be read out loud at the meeting again. We were asked if we could provide the Emergency Service, staff the call centre in Control with our members "triaging" or prioritising emergencies from the public and then relaying them to the crews waiting at the station. This caused quite a debate especially as members who had not attended the previous meeting about withdrawing from outpatients had to live with the consequences. Once again, Roger the branch secretary read us out the letter, although the network of stewards already knew the content.

Following the chaos from the last meeting, Roger was very keen to get back on track this time but could not help anticipate the Chief's reaction to the proposal. We listened intently as we knew that he and the Chief were close. Roger made it clear that the Chief would have none of this and would never give up control of the whole operation to the unions and sit on the sidelines and watch. He knew that the Chief was busy finalising plans with the police and military for the "What If?" scenario, the one that everyone talked about but made sure nobody heard: "What If ...they go on strike?" Even though Roger seemed forthright and stubbornly opinionated around union matters he had an academic side that he kept well hidden and was one of the first fully qualified paramedics in the UK, something for which we admired him. He was also an inspiration when I was crewed with him as he had a brilliant bedside manner with patients and an infectious laugh.

It seemed strange that we were already in work attending all emergencies, sometimes with better levels of cover around the clock than would have been rostered but were still having this savage 30% cut in wages. The offer to run our own service was a long shot but attempted to keep management away from the day to day running and get the service to hand its whole operation lock, stock and barrel to us and our members. Amazingly, in some areas - including our neighbours like Gwent - they did just that, the Chiefs having talks with the reps about rotas to maintain a 999 service. The point was that we were to receive calls direct from the public even though no overtime was being used in answering only emergency calls. At this point some crews (notably those in London) began refusing to answer any calls from central control. They dealt only with emergency calls made directly to stations by the public or hospitals. In Sandwell, in the Midlands, the Labour council was running a semi-official alternative service which was being reported on and watched very carefully by the union.

We were about to demand the same position in our service, though we were aware that another Service had cut the phone lines to the Stations and we had to consider these responses especially as the same strategy may have been used on us. In various parts of the country more crews had been suspended, and the army and the police had put the contingency plans into action by running a limited ambulance service. Some of our members either lived near, or were, members of the Territorial Army.

The Field Ambulance had a division in Cardiff barracks where Keith Menzies, Gerry Owen and Roy Barry who worked on our station were based.
We also had members who were Special Police Officers. They witnessed the arrival and storage of the "green goddesses" at the camp and were party to the contingency plans that were being drawn up in conjunction with the army and the police in the event of an escalation of the dispute. The Chief failed to mention to anyone his links with St John Ambulance but he had struck a gentleman's agreement with their boss, Doug (who, at one time, used to work with us and whose twin daughters were in my class at school) and they were to be the first line of defence.

By the following day - as Roger accurately predicted - we found that our Chief was having none of it. He told us that we were going too far, even though we were virtually at the point that was being proposed anyway, with our members in Control not actually losing money but broadly sympathetic to the fate of the road staff by that time. In practice there was a polarisation around what real 999 emergencies were, following weeks of attempts to upgrade routine outpatient visits to emergency status. Consequently colleagues in Control seemed to use much more discretion and not send crews out unless it was to a real emergency, whereas before everybody who rang 999 automatically received the benefit of a fully manned ambulance for however trivial a call.

The Chief said he would take action to prevent us running the service ourselves. We also understood that personal relationships with the Chief and union reps (apart from Roger) were strained so, over many hours, Roger tried to persuade the Chief not to make any rash decisions. The responses were courteous, although an insider informed us they could hear raised voices from the office. I have to believe the accounts because I was kept well away from the discussions with the Chief. When we were told he would take steps, we knew he was a man of his word and he would investigate. In researching this matter I have seen the internal letters attempting to avert action at two crucial stages. In a letter to GMB, the Chief described how unacceptable he finds the "National Trade Union Proposals" that staff should not take instructions from any staff who have not had their pay abated. He then went on to state:

> We have given careful consideration to this ultimatum and have sought appropriate advice from our legal Advisors. Advice so far received indicates that such action on behalf of your members might well be construed as 'strike action' and if proceeded with could prove to be contrary to the legislation in the absence of a strike ballot. It is therefore our view that threat of this action should be withdrawn immediately and that staff should continue to accept instructions from Officers and staff irrespective of whether their pay has been abated or not.

In a further personal letter to staff the Chief stated that he would modify the abatement of salary to re-instate 100% of pay to the emergency crews and pay 75% of the outpatient crews' salary if we could consider "a resumption of patient transport services to day hospital cases. Flexibility by day staff in dealing with non emergency discharges and transfers would increase their pay to 85%". It was all getting a bit muddy, abatements of 15%, 25%, 30% and 100% were proposed if we would lift what the Chief decided were the key sanctions affecting the Service. Whilst staff were not in the best of moods to contemplate any of the abatements and responses to the service, it was clear that things were getting complicated. He went on to state that

> I have advised the Trade Unions that I am prohibiting the use of any NHS facilities and resources in seeking to set up "the alternative Ambulance Service referred to in Trade Unions instructions. Failure to adhere to this instruction will result in the immediate issue of a Writ and application to the High Court for an injunction to prevent any such use.

He then finished his letter with a more conciliatory tone saying "provided that the threat of escalation on Thursday is withdrawn, I am prepared to agree to a joint approach to ACAS to request their facilities in mediation and conciliation of this local issue." It had become a blinking contest locally. Neighbouring crews from the adjoining counties had struck a deal with their Chiefs to run the service locally. It was very hard for our Chief, who we all had a fondness for, to extrapolate the local issues from the national ones. It seemed bizarre that we had a Chief who, even though exerting his authority, would offer to break the deadlock by agreeing to go to ACAS locally, while at national level the officials and politicians were refusing that offer from the trade unions to do just the same.

Our argument was not with the Chief Ambulance Officer or our colleagues in the adjoining counties or the St.John or the Police or the Army, it was with the Secretary of State for Health who was dictating Government policy to NHS Department of Health civil servants to stay firm and solid on the matter of pay. Having prior notice of the intention of serving a Writ followed with a High Court injunction there were some more behind the scenes discussions that took place late into the night at the Headquarters building. Within days the Chief was on the train to London to administer hundreds of injunctions in the High Court. Most of us sensed his resolve. We just did not expect him to act so quickly.

Chapter 7: The High Court injunction

Before the end of the week of the issue of the union letter to branches, the subsequent meeting to vote on our proposal to run the service and the reaction of the Chief, we had received news that our neighbouring counties were beginning to run the services themselves and were effectively in the handover period from management. We had previously heard news reports that on 11th November the London Ambulance crews had been suspended and there were suggestions made in the House of Commons by Shadow Health Spokesman, Robin Cook MP that other services were planning similar responses to this latest stage of the dispute.

I was home that Friday afternoon, I remember the knock on the door. Dave Rumbelow was one of the few uniformed managers in the service that I highly respected - mostly because he was so honest and easy to deal with and had so much integrity. A quietly spoken man, he stood at my door, his six foot three inch frame bending forward and outstretched, he handed me a letter in a brown envelope. "I'm sorry I have to do this and bring you this. I'm supposed to serve it on you and not just hand it to you", he said. I looked up at his face as I read the terms of the injunction from the High Court in London and asked him: "Are we all having one of these, or just the Union reps or what?"

"Everyone's having one", he replied, "I've got another 30 odd in the car to deliver, sorry serve on, people. It's going to take me all night." As he walked away I could tell that he was very saddened to have to do this duty. Of course, before I had the chance to ring anyone to warn them what was about to be delivered, my neighbour Les (who had been in the Service about 10 years longer than I had) was at the door checking if I had just received what he did. We chatted and although we had an idea that the Chief had gone to London, we assumed it was for advice from Counsel - not to have the injunctions written up and brought back on the train that afternoon.

When we spoke it dawned on me that the bloody books were kept in the locker on station and that I would have to get them out. So we drove down to the station, the ink still not dried on the injunction, with its first line about preventing us entering any service premises. On station there were quite a few officers in a state of confusion: some knew what the implications of the injunction meant and what it was designed for, while some seemed oblivious. Luckily one of them was Ralph Knight a man who had a great affinity with the road staff. On Christmas Day every year he turned up like clockwork with a few packs of cigarettes for the crews working. The same brand, Benson and Hedges at the same time, every Christmas day since the mid 1970s. It demonstrated that he had not forgotten he was one of us. Ralph let me in and covered the situation with his colleagues whilst I got the books. Ralph explained that a couple of staff had got word early that the injunction was on its way and had reported in sick, legally avoiding the injunction. When I had the books in my hand, little did I think that I would not be setting foot officially in the station again for months. Driving home I diverted past the barracks and saw on the yard through the fence that the Army staff were revving up the green goddesses ready for deployment the following day. I realised there and then that I would not be going in for my next shift to answer 999 calls. It also started to dawn on me that I would not be getting any pay.

Chapter 8: Light the brazier

Strike paraphernalia is not readily available on the high street. Braziers and megaphones are specialist items. Yet by the first day, all of us had made the decision to come in and there was a brazier burning at the car park space at the top of the drive to the station. Within a couple of days we also had a caravan, a late 'sixties model that looked like the ones from the *Carry On Camping* film. We bought it from an uncle of one of our members. Only a few pounds changed hands and it was soon parked in such a way that the stable door faced outwards into the car park, making it Dispute HQ.

On the very first day of standing out we must have looked like a pretty mystified bunch, virtually none of us knew what to do and the caravan had not yet arrived. But the Fire Service colleagues from the Fire Brigades Union turned up, having just been to the cash and carry warehouse, and donated to us half of their week's supply of meat, mostly sausages, bacon and chops. We had not figured out how to adapt the brazier to use as a cooker although as it was already lit and red hot. Of course we had no fridge and no cooker. Somehow we had to get in the station. At lunchtime an officer in a car came back to the station and we did not consider that they were crossing a picket line as we had been locked out and turned up blindly to the station in a loosely organised way. So the bacon was taken in to the station and the station officer - who clearly did not have an injunction - was bribed with a bacon sandwich and the mass catering exercise took place for the first time.

We realised on day one that if we were expecting staff to come to the station, do a bit of parading with placards and then walk the half a mile or so past the Welsh Office to the vantage points we had determined were best to maximise the monies that were flowing in to the buckets, then really we had to feed them. An army marches on its stomach. The brazier was the worst type of barbeque imaginable with the fuel sourced from branches of trees and bushes that stretched into the dirty canal feeder under the bridge. The food and waste wood was mostly donated, sometimes a member of the public or one of the spouses or relatives would bring a tupperware donation full of home- made pastries and the toaster in the caravan was constantly on and its cupboards packed with cereal (mostly Weetabix). Tea and coffee was on tap and we had plenty of polystyrene cups. Like every ambulance station there was never any sugar.

We had set up regular collection points and were vigilant enough to staff them constantly during office and shopping hours. I stayed on at the brazier on the first night not knowing what time we should go home. My sister's boss Waldo owned an Italian restaurant in the city centre (my Mum is Italian from the vicinity of the ankle in the South) named after his town near Rome and that night, like many future nights, he stopped by in his Mercedes and dropped off boxes of freshly cooked pizza, enough for everyone there. The sight of a police van arriving at the drive on the first night was a bit chilling, as I spent two seconds thinking, "have we broken any laws here?" I was convinced we had not when the two coppers jumped out and came straight up to us. They proceeded to tell us how many "ambulance" 999 calls they had been sent to since they came on duty that lunchtime. They said how scary it was when someone was ill, maybe even having a heart attack and they didn't have any knowledge, training or equipment to deal with it. Then they showed us the back of the van which only had the bench seat that the prisoners sat on the night before and on the floor a few blankets and pillows for the worst cases.

I was annoyed at that stage with the Chief for rushing the decision to lock us out and allow the only service to people in my city to be as poor or worse than a third world country would have. In our neighbouring authorities and services the Chiefs had not quite handed over the service to the crews but worked together in a co-operative way to facilitate the staff themselves to run the service with the safety net of a couple of people (officers) just down the corridor if they were needed. It was a smoke and mirrors difference to an ordinary Ambulance Service, cosmetic almost but we weren't going to have that option, even on a trial basis as I had suggested. We were well and truly locked out. We could see the green goddesses on the streets and outside Casualty at the hospital and we regularly spoke to the police who all said the same thing "I couldn't do your job mate, well not permanently anyway". On about the third day a storm was whipping up and we must have had the world record for numbers crammed in a caravan when a police van turned up at the picket line at the top of the drive. The driver jumped out of the van and said that there had been an incident near the theatre where the wind had whipped down the road where the tower blocks were and ripped a huge wooden hoarding off its stand and it had landed on a bus stop injuring over a dozen people. There were hardly any coppers to deal with it and he was on his way down there and asked if one person could go down with him to make sure they were doing everything right. All the assembled pickets jumped on the van and the outpatient vehicles parked up at the top of the drive behind the woodsheds.

Officially they had broken the injunction there and then. The police officer explained that the injuries varied between severe head injuries and cuts to the legs. The pickets treated the injured alongside the army and the police, took the patients to hospital, handed over the symptoms to the nurses at the Infirmary and then jumped back in the vehicles, drove them back and parked them up at the station behind the woodshed and put the keys in the keypress under the supervision of the officer. His only job on the station during those first few days was to stay on station in case a member of the public was unaware that the lock out and injunctions existed and needed the assistance of an ambulance. Then these randomly assembled crews walked back up the drive until they reached the top where they joined their colleagues who were on the picket line, all the while reminding themselves that they were not on strike and that they did not cross a picket line because we were all locked out. No action was ever taken against these good Samaritans.

Nobody was trying to go into work as we were all locked out, universally, even the ones who would have gone in to work if they had a choice. The injunction was indiscriminate, it applied to all road based staff and it caused some anger that operational senior officers were still receiving their pay and performing mostly office based and control duties. Ralph Knight and Ken Healey were two officers who stood out on the picket line with the road staff. There were a handful of those who made enough noise about disagreeing with what had happened to them to alert us to the fact that there were those who would drop everything if they were asked to help the army and there was a small minority who were asking if there was some way they could work. They were not put in the class of good Samaritan.

Chapter 9: The petition

Word was out that there was a petition to support the case of ambulance staff and within a couple of days we all had our own copies to be filled in. That took very little effort as we had them at every collection point and they drew the public like magnets. Although we asked the public to sign the petition just once that didn't stop people coming back on a weekly, sometimes daily, basis to throw a few coins into the bucket. They were always rewarded with a sticker that stated "Support The Ambulance Workers". The placards were strategically held by our staff on the roadside parade that we had developed into theatre and we would be very keen to get a line of six equally spaced apart at the same distance from the kerb: one male, one female, one younger, one older at key times of the day and we would sometimes take the format on tour to arterial routes.

We always had buckets on the picket lines and collection points but once we got the "Sign Our Petition" placards we had to create a pull in off the road so that drivers could stop and sign and sometimes have a chat or a catch up; they were all welcome. We noticed that the slicker we became at the placards, the better the response even though there had been a few minor road accidents at the nearby junction that I have to admit we caused by distracting drivers too much. We never received any hassle or pressure to move from the police -

probably because they were in the back of the police van with patients. Occasionally in the shopping centre, maybe twice a day, a person would stroll up and tell us to "get back to work". If they would stay and play, we explained that we were locked out and could not go back to work even if we tried without breaking the terms of the High Court injunction. That generally deflated the average critic although more than once I was told that we brought all of our problems upon ourselves and nobody could win a battle with Margaret Thatcher. We would politely explain that we did not want to personalise it and we were not on an anti-government dispute. Although some Tory supporters chose not to agree with us, we had a case that the average person did at least follow once explained. We also would add that we needed a mechanism to ensure a pay dispute never happened again.

A couple of us were on the "lecture and collection" list and could collect hundreds of signatures in one lunchtime in one location. By the time 15th December 1989 arrived and it was handed in to Parliament, there were over 4.5 million signatures with another 500,000 missing the deadline. They had to set up special storage in the basement of the House of Commons and use six ambulance stretchers to carry the boxes in. It was the biggest petition ever undertaken and handed in to Parliament. We discovered it had become the biggest petition in the world and was to be included in the Guinness Book of Records. The presentation of the petition was timed to coincide with a debate in Parliament on the dispute on the 15th December 1989. Robin Cook, the Shadow Secretary of State for Health, opened the debate saying:

> It is the largest petition presented to Parliament since the new rules were devised 150 years ago. The petition reads: that the Ambulance dispute is in need of urgent resolution. Wherefore your Petitioners pray that your honourable House urge the Secretary of State for Health to use the good offices of ACAS and agree to arbitration in order to end this unnecessary dispute: and urge the Secretary of State to provide a pay formula for the Ambulance Service similar to that for the other emergency services. The record size of the petition is a powerful statement of public support for the dedication and courage of ambulance staff. It shows the public dismay that they are still denied arbitration. Its presentation is timely in that it comes just before the busiest week in the year for this vital emergency service. I appeal to the

> House and to the Government to listen to this magnificent plea by the public, who need their ambulance service, for a just and urgent settlement to the dispute.

The ongoing debate had nothing to do with the content of the petition itself but derision towards Robin Cook for overshadowing some of the minor petitions also to be handed in that day and the fact that he had brought six stretchers into the chamber when he could have just brought one or two sample pages. Tony Benn jumped in to defend him by extolling the history of petitions and what the King's view of them might be (although he didn't specify which King) and added

> I do not wish to give offence to you, Mr. Speaker ; I wish to assert an ancient right. The fact is that three quarters of a million people who signed that petition believing that it would be presented physically to Parliament have been told today that, because of the business of the House, it cannot be brought in. If 4.5 million people had signed a petition in Prague or Warsaw, all the news media in Britain would have featured programmes about it for a week.

Chapter 10: New Year, 'glorified taxi drivers' and the debate in Parliament

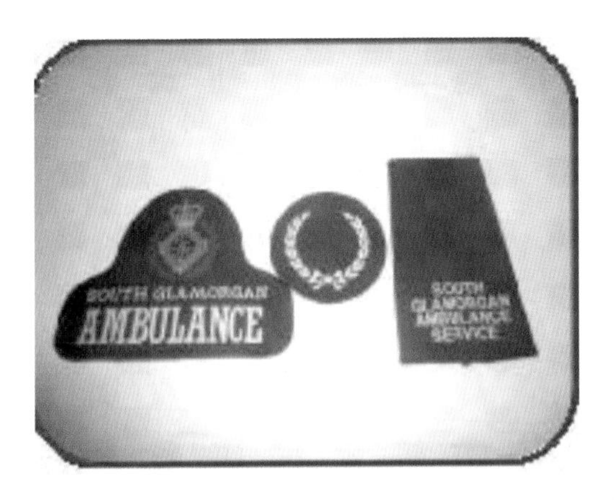

Christmas had been pretty bleak; Building Societies advertised that ambulance staff who were facing financial difficulties could come into the branch and freeze their mortgages with no financial penalty. Quite a few of us took up that offer. The staff who had children were worried that they could not buy presents for them and an appeal was launched where toys were collected and distributed around the country from a central point at the HQ in Waterloo of the London Ambulance Service. A Christmas card was produced by the joint unions to be sent to Kenneth Clarke urging him not to be a Scrooge. The cartoon was by Steve Bell the political cartoonist at the *Guardian* newspaper.

.

Around January 1990 a huge row broke out in Parliament and the debates that followed give a revealing insight into the pressure building up politically at the beginning of 1990. Kenneth Clarke was alleged to have made reference to ambulance staff as taxi drivers. The remark is disputed, but what is clear is that when Kenneth Clarke responded by letter to a constituent, the leaking of it provoked a lot of offence because of Clarke's tone and the way he described ambulance staff. It became even more offensive when it was revealed that it was in response to a letter received from the 15 year old daughter of an ambulance worker. Kenneth Clarke wrote:

> The vast majority of ambulance staff have had no extended paramedical training at all. They are professional drivers, a worthwhile job-but not an exceptional one."

Around the same time, a debate was scheduled in Parliament on the dispute. The debate in the House of Commons on the 11th January 1990[1] was dominated by Robin Cook who started the debate by saying:

> I beg to move, That this House recognises that ambulance staff provide an essential emergency service; notes that four-fifths of all ambulance crews are fully qualified to provide skilled attention to the casualties of accidents and to patients with critical medical conditions and that many of the others are recent recruits; records its appreciation of the commitment staff have shown to the ambulance service and the courage they have often displayed at the scene of accidents; is conscious of the overwhelming public support for a just pay award to ambulance staff and for a pay mechanism to avoid disruption of this emergency service in future years; expresses its dismay that the current industrial dispute has remained unresolved for four months; and calls upon Her Majesty's Government to commence early negotiations to secure a settlement. Those words record our recognition of the commitment and dedication of the ambulance service. They call for an urgent settlement of the dispute. There is not a breath of criticism in those words of the Secretary of State. The right hon. and learned Gentleman will well understand that that being the case, the motion does not express my innermost thoughts about his conduct in office. I read in the newspapers—in some surprising newspapers these days—that the Secretary of State is thought to have got himself into a hole. I must advise my hon. Friends that our duty on this occasion is to throw down ropes to the right hon. and learned Gentleman and, heavy though the burden may be, haul him up until he is within reach of a settlement. If that disappoints my hon. Friends, I assure them that there will be plenty of occasions in the future when they can shove him back down the hole.

---

[1] The extensive quotations from Hansard used in this section are reproduced under Parliamentary licence.

He then elaborated by describing the pay offer

> I shall return to the management's allegedly improved offer later in my speech. That improved offer would mean converting 6.5 per cent over 12 months into 9 per cent over 18 months. I doubt if even the offensive, aggressive and, I read in the article from which I quoted, disgusting and disgraceful Minister for the Environment and Countryside would try to claim that there was a substantial difference between 6.5 per cent over 12 months and 9 per cent over 18 months. But I do not expect to see the Minister for the Environment and Countryside voting with us at the end of the debate.
>
> Nor do we table this motion of studied moderation in the hope that Conservative Members will vote with us. I have stood at the Dispatch Box often enough to know that if I were to move, "That this January is warmer than usual", that motion would be voted down because it was moved by the Opposition. Indeed, the hon. Member for Harlow (Mr. Hayes) would probably have intervened by now to disagree with me. Therefore, I do not expect Conservative Members to join us in the Lobby tonight, but I ask them to speak for their constituents in this debate and to express the public view.

He proceeded to explain that the Prime Minister had previously written in a letter whilst Leader of the Opposition that she thought then that the Ambulance Service was an emergency service:

> I hope that Conservative Members will treat the debate as a debate about a service in crisis. That service is an emergency service. I repeat that it is an emergency service. The crisis in that service has left people lying in pain and distress for longer than any civilised society should tolerate. It has left people in a state of collapse without the skilled treatment that they need at the point when they are attended.
>
> The Government's amendment expresses appreciation of the police and the Army. I have no doubt whatsoever that thousands of policemen and service men in the past four months have given of their best to

> provide the best cover that they can. But if we are serious in appreciating what they have done, we must listen to what they say to us about the cover that they can provide.
>
> We must listen, for instance, to Mike Bennett, the chairman of the Metropolitan police branch of the Police Federation, who has stated: At the end of the day apart from being totally unqualified to run an efficient service, we are using vehicles which really any self-respecting prisoner would complain about, let alone a patient. We have a standing instruction not to convey people with head injuries in police vehicles, and yet here we are doing it. The vehicles are not designed for this ... they are designed for carrying goods not people ... If the money is there why can't it go to solving the dispute? There are plenty of cases on record to show that the emergency service that has been brought in as a substitute for the ambulance service cannot cope with emergency calls.

Cook noted that the Secretary of State contests the claim that the ambulance service is an emergency service on the basis that emergency cases represent just one in 10 of all patients carried. Cook says that he has

> tried to find out where that figure comes from. It is not an easy figure to find. In a parliamentary question on 19 December, the Secretary of State was asked if he would estimate the average time spent by an ambulanceman on transporting (a) emergency cases and (b) non-emergency cases. The Minister's answer to the question was: "This information is not available". Where does that figure of one in 10 come from?

In a partial answer to his own question, Cook reports that he has the figures for London for the first nine months of last year—the period before the dispute, and that

> They show that, of calls to the London ambulance service in the first nine months of last year, the number of emergency cases was not one in 10 but one in four. I repeat the question: where does the figure of

> one in 10 come from? If that figure is to be the basis for comparison, can we have the figures for the other two emergency services?

Cook then compared these figures with the police. Using a study of the Merseyside police – what he described as 'the most comprehensive study of how police spend their time' – he showed that the police spent 9% of their time responding to crime incidents, 1% responding to traffic incidents and 2% responding to other incidents. This is a total of 12% of their time spent responding to incidents, not all of which were emergencies. Cook remarked:

> I would not for one moment suggest that the police are not an emergency service. It would defy common sense to suggest that. However, by the same token, it defies common sense to tell ambulance crews that they are not an emergency service. On Monday night, the nation had the opportunity to witness the professional and competent response of the ambulance service to the emergency caused by the pile-up on the M25, when six crews, who have not been paid since October, responded to an emergency call to treat victims of acute injuries. Few hon. Members could look on those injuries, far less know how to begin to rescue the victims. Those crews know that they are an emergency service, and they are mystified and wounded that the Health Service is in the hands of a Secretary of State who tries to deny it.

He referred to a letter written by the Secretary of State in which he referred to ambulance staff as professional drivers and which he had accused COHSE of quoting out of context. Cook said:

> I understand that the Secretary of State is sensitive on that point… Therefore, to avoid any doubt, I shall read the full paragraph. In context, the statement reads no better than it does out of context. Frankly, in the context of a letter to a 15-year-old girl about her father, it reads decidedly worse than when it is taken out of context.
>
> The letter states: The vast majority— I ask the House to remember those words— of ambulance staff have had no extended paramedical training at all. They are professional drivers, a worthwhile job —but not

an exceptional one. It is clear beyond reasonable doubt from the context that the Secretary of State is describing the vast majority of qualified ambulance staff as professional drivers. Four out of five ambulance staff are fully qualified. That means that they are trained in life-saving skills, can treat head injuries and those with spinal injuries and open wounds. All the fully qualified ambulance staff are trained in resuscitation and the suction of blockages. All of them are capable of carrying out childbirths in emergencies. In their career many ambulance staff have carried out more than 50 births at the kerbside. They are all trained in handling and lifting people with serious fractures. Many of them put themselves at risk in providing those services to accident victims.

The ambulance personnel who responded to the pile-up on the M25 drove through the same thick fog that caused that pile-up and attended the victims in that thick fog. Those ambulance staff who attended some Conservative Members in the Grand hotel did so while one floor of it collapsed.

Increasingly, those ambulance staff are being assaulted by those they come to serve. I have here a letter sent by an ambulance man in Barnsley. It states: I have had my spectacles smashed on two occasions ... I have been kicked and abused and, on one occasion, threatened with a shotgun ... Who is more at risk these days than the ambulanceman from contracting A.I.D.S., or Hepatitis B ... We don't stop to ask the injured and dying patient if he is suffering with these diseases—we just get on with doing what has to be done. That is the job that the Secretary of State describes as "worthwhile" but "not exceptional". What professional driver needs those skills, takes those risks and undergoes that stress?

The Secretary of State and his Department know about the stress on ambulance drivers. Seven years ago it received a report on stress among ambulance workers. It was a report in the context of a study on whether ambulance staff should be allowed to retire earlier than at 65 years of age. That study found that few made it to the retirement age of 65. Most took early retirement, frequently through ill health. Of the few

> who made it to 65, the average period of survival in retirement was 2.4 years. We are haggling over a pay award to a group of workers whose mortality rate is one quarter higher than the average for industrial workers.
>
> In the negotiations, to quote the Secretary of State's letter to Miss Mitchell, we are told the union side has not budged an inch. Since the dispute began, the staff side has dropped its demands for enhanced payments for overtime, standby payments to staff on call, an increment for long service and a reduction in working hours. The only two elements that remain are for a higher pay award this year—and staff are willing to compromise on the amount—and for a pay mechanism for future years—and staff are willing to compromise on the formula.

Cook pointed to pay settlement data that showed the offer to ambulance staff was much less than pay settlements elsewhere, including the 10.6% pay award to MPs. In his reply, Clarke referred to 'remarks that I was alleged to have made about ambulance men'. He defended his performance during the dispute, repeating his view that the ambulance staff pay claim was 'excessive', the management offer 'fair and generous' and the industrial action 'unjustified' – 'as industrial action in any essential service cannot be justified' (without mentioning that 999 essential services were actually being covered). Despite numbers of MPs pointing to the high levels of skill and training of many ambulance staff, and the fact that a lack of Government funding was the main reason holding back the further training and deployment of paramedics, Clarke was unrepentant and refused to apologise for the letter in which he described ambulance staff as professional drivers.

Chapter 11: BBC Week In Week Out

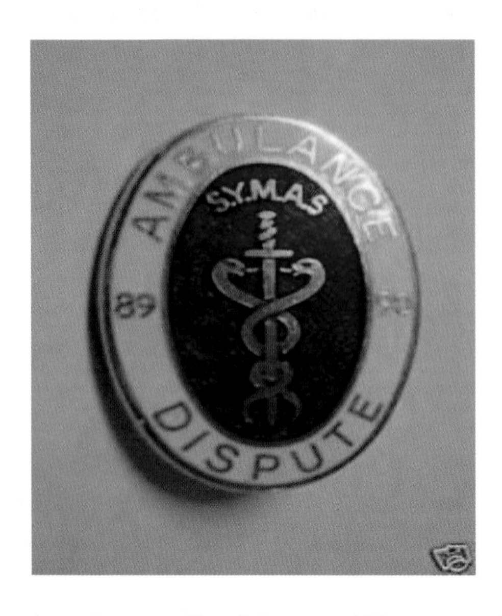

By the late 1980s quite a few satellite dishes could be seen adorning houses in virtually every street and Sky News had recently launched a 24 hour news service that broke many of the stories relating to the dispute as they were happening. Having 24 hours to fill each day, they also had film crews decamped to the frontline interviewing suspended or locked out crews on a regular basis for updates without ever using the word "strike" in their reporting.

ITV had a serious national and local news slot just after Fred the Weatherman jumped around the map in Liverpool's Albert Dock at the end of Richard and Judy's *This Morning* programme. Reports by the Health correspondent Peter Cullimore were always clear and relevant to the latest developments. Televising Parliament was a recent innovation and the novelty of this often meant that for the first time, the public could see the MPs debating issues regarding the ambulance dispute.

I had been told by someone who had insight and was very authoritative on the subject that the BBC had a bias against strikers related to the fact that their own staff had pulled the plug on more than one occasion.

I could not concur with this sweeping generalisation from my experience of the BBC journalists, which started early during October 1989 mostly with local radio. There seemed to be a streamlined approach to news gathering and a few key writers had a "hold the front page" arrangement with their editors and it was clear who they were. Whenever one of those stories was written it would invariably be followed up by radio and T.V. Once we were a month or so into the dispute, the novelty of the press visiting with the obligatory Marantz tape machines with attached microphones had worn off for us at grassroots level. We made a conscious effort at all times to stay on message and carefully controlled who stepped up to speak or appear.

BBC Wales had a well known investigative reporter who brought to every story he covered, the gravitas and experience of a very serious man indeed. His name was Vincent Kane. My Dad knew him as they quite often attended the same pub at the same time, usually after Church. Vincent Kane would be wheeled out for very serious documentaries and had a reputation for being hard hitting yet nimble enough on his feet to host live television debates.

One such debate was organised as soon as the St. John Ambulance, the army and the police were on the streets of the capital. Roger reluctantly agreed to do the programme as branch secretary of the biggest union in membership. There was no opposition at branch level to this decision. We all watched at 10.00 p.m. when the lights of the studio floor gently lit up to show just two chairs: Roger sat in one and the Chief in the other, opposite each other with Mr Kane stood like a colossus between them. Vincent Kane introduced the subject with a quick resume of the origins of the dispute as the screen cut to the footage of the police struggling to cope with a patient in the back of a van and scenes of ambulance staff locked out of the stations. Cutting back to the studio he laid the blame for the events squarely at the feet of the Chief for not allowing staff to answer calls from the public. The Chief struggled to convince the presenter that there was any other side to this and he was reminded that geographically there was much better cover and less of a consequence elsewhere in the Principality as a result of the decisions of the other Chiefs who had made a pact with their staff. "So you have no faith in your staff running a good service?" he accused the Chief who just couldn't answer. The camera lingered on him in silence whilst Mr Kane considered his next question from the pad snuggled into his armpit which contained the next lethal weapon.

Kane then painted a scenario in which one of his family may be injured on the street outside his house and he has to wait until either a St John's, Green Goddess or police van rolled up. Nobody interrupted him as very few people ever had. The Chief was lost for words and luckily Roger didn't have to say much even though we had had a rehearsal of what was likely to be asked which did not materialise. The programme was very damaging locally to the employers and was a pivotal point in our campaign as before then the human cost had never been spelt out. Previously, reports had emphasised the industrial dispute aspects.

Chapter 12: BBC2 Newsnight

Newsnight was on every weeknight on BBC2 at 10.30pm. and was essential viewing for reps in the dispute. Word had come to the NUPE office that they wanted a uniformed rep from a branch that was clearly locked out to come to London for a televised TV debate involving staff affected by the dispute and politicians.

By this time a leaflet had been produced detailing which services were suspended, locked out or working. Obviously a bit bruised from his close encounter with Vincent Kane a few weeks earlier, Roger was reluctant and suggested that, as I had the "spokesperson" role, I should do it. Luckily Sonia's cousin Julia was studying Law in London so I had a place to stay in Woodford. I was to call at the NUPE office to collect my fare in cash. It barely covered the coach fare never mind a train and, as I had often did, I walked in uniform to the bus station.

On the coach to Victoria when settled into my seat I could see that my reversible semi reflective coat was showing signs of wear and dirt from weeks in front of the brazier and my shoes could do with replacing from before the start of the summer. It did seem strange making my way to Broadcasting House in rush hour in my uniform ready for 7pm which I thought was extremely early in the evening for Newsnight.

Once ushered into the green room by very supportive BBC staff in uniform that was much smarter than mine, I met the other contributors. We sat and talked and I heard that London, Surrey, Liverpool had similar issues to mine and we tried to decide who would be best placed to articulate any commonality. There was a panel of about 18 or 20 of us and some of them didn't say a word in the green room, not a word in run through rehearsal without any politicians and it soon dawned on me that it was going to be recorded at about 8.00p.m. and not live at all.

The politicians were Robin Cook, the Shadow Health Spokesman and Ann Widdecombe who was junior Minister at the Department of Health. She wasn't very friendly to him, us or the presenter Donald MacCormick. When we got underway she must have won the world record for sipping water as she was asked immediately "Where is Mr Clarke?" "He is very busy" she replied. "Obviously not sorting out this ambulance dispute" said Mr MacCormick, usually a more polite and diplomatic journalist than his opposite number Mr Paxman. He asked for a regional round up from the assembled uniformed posse of activists which clearly seemed to intimidate Ms Widdecombe as she did not lift her head from the glass to gaze at any one of us during the whole hour of recording.

Retiring to the green room afterwards I was approached by a member of staff who gave me a brown envelope with a window in it containing £30 which was my appearance fee and expenses. I explained that I had a coach fare and was staying with my cousin. He insisted I had it anyway and said to take the train home and get a good meal. Robin Cook came in the room and shook everyone's hand, briefly chatting with all. Ann Widdecombe left without speaking to any NHS Staff.

Out on the street in the cold, we all said a quick goodbye to each other and I realised that I had to journey to South Woodford to stay on the exact opposite side of London which would take me just over half the time it would have to return home. I arrived at Julia's with a couple of minutes to spare and we settled in to watch Newsnight. Virtually every section that had my small contribution had been edited out, the vision of Ann Widdecombe in her sipping contest was edited out and anything slightly inflammatory or beginning with the words "This Government" was kept in.

However it was here that I first heard the word "intransigence" related to the tactic of not moving from a rigid approach, especially after there had been suggestions that the Government were trying to "starve us out". Robin Cook was brilliant at stating chapter and verse on how much this dispute had cost the British people and that running the service with the army and police was costing more than it would have cost to settle the dispute. He went on to say that we needed a review body or formula so this type of dispute could never happen again, when Ann Widdecombe disagreed, he reminded her that MPs had one and they had not even asked for it.

There was to be another memorable ambulance moment on Newsnight a few weeks later when Kenneth Clarke appeared live. Sitting at the desk and watching the video tape, Jeremy Paxman turned to him and said: "You've made rather a mess of handling this dispute haven't you?" Not so much of a question, more a statement. Newsnight also conducted a poll which gave us overwhelming public support even amongst Tory voters. In one of their editorials they said:

> This is a public relations triumph...the battle for public support has been won, for now at least by the unions. A Government which once seemed the master of P.R. has been beaten at its own game.
> (Newsnight,18th December 1989)

There may have been a conspiracy from some of the hierarchy at the BBC towards or against strikers during the mid nineteen-eighties but I didn't feel it at any time against us.

Chapter 13: 75,000 on the march and rally

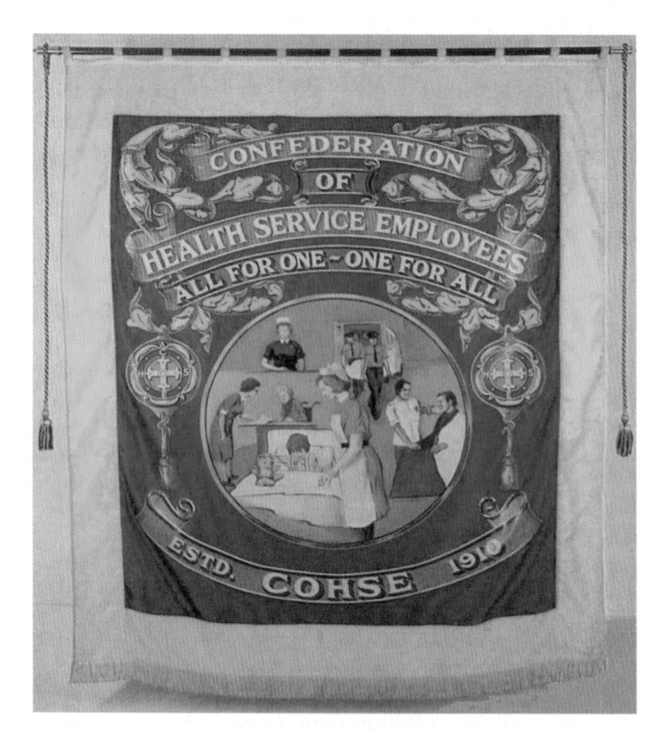

There was a date set for a march and rally scheduled to end in Trafalgar Square, London on Saturday 13th January 1990. Once it became known that there were coaches and the chance of a free train, everyone wanted to go. The fact that we did not have to organise that much apart from getting everyone at the rendezvous points by 7a.m. was a great relief. There had been a build up to the march in the press including accounts a couple of days before on Thursday 11th of the Parliamentary debate of the dispute. There were expected to be large numbers on the march - not just of affected ambulance staff and their families but from supporters of the cause in other trade unions and the general public.

There was a percolation of resentment from some crews around the country as it was clear that some services were still working normally while others were pressing for escalation with growing national press interest. Of course I jumped on the train.

It felt strange getting off the mainline train then walking to the tube platform as the whole of the London Underground network seemed to be swarming with ambulance uniforms, each station stop receiving some more until we all reached our destination, a sight quite surreal. We were to be sorted into regions and slots in the mass assembly on the embankment according to our area and union. However the numbers were so overwhelming that I couldn't believe so many would be there from every trade union you've ever heard of and plenty I hadn't: students, political activists, members of the public, patient groups, WRVS, and the most humbling presence, pensioners groups. It was an amazing feeling to be surrounded by so many people who believed in us.

It was in these couple of days between the march and the petition that the first reports of "wildcat" strike action were reported. This is where crews walk out with no ballot or ability to provide emergency cover or give notice to the employer as it is a flare up usually related to events that by-pass all of the "normal" processes of industrial relations or a trade dispute. The talk of these unofficial walk outs beginning to materialise came as we were stood in line waiting to march under our banners that morning. Whilst we spoke with each other amongst the different services it was clear that members were angry the way the dispute had progressed. We were having arguments and leaflets and articles thrust into our hands by various participants and it felt as we started off through the streets that something was brewing.

We tried to stick together both during the march and the subsequent rally at Trafalgar Square. It was a relief, for one day at least, not to worry about having to carry buckets and all the responsibility surrounding collecting, as before we had even arrived at London it was decided that all collections on this day were to be for the London crews. We had the freedom from buckets to end up in the pub just close to Whitehall after the rally. We found that we did not have to put our hands in our pockets to buy a drink for the short time we were there before scheduled departure time. I was amazed that I bumped into my mate from training school, John based in Brighton.

Chapter 14: The Day (or at least 15 minutes) of Action

The TUC planned a national 15 minute stoppage all over the UK with a quarter of an hour's pay to be donated to the ambulance staff. Some groups including the Socialist Workers Party and the Workers' Voice were pushing that this should be a national strike. As the collection committee of three of us discussed collecting opportunities I was given the job of going through the various requests we had for speakers and collectors to visit workplaces.

I was delighted that the unions at my old employer the Department of Trade at Companies House had requested my presence at midday on January 30th. I walked up to the building with two buckets and was going to be picked up at 12.30p.m. by Roger Leismeier from GMB, an absolute gentleman who was quietly spoken and wanted to be there to support me. On this occasion I brought the megaphone with the curly lead and mouthpiece more for the effect than necessity.

So many people had congregated in the huge canteen that the security herded us out into the car park where I stood on a raised plant bed to make my address. It was an amazing reaction as I explained that there was much more to the dispute than had been written in the press. I had a huge round of applause and the two buckets rapidly filled up with cash.

I was especially delighted to see my great friend Gail Richards and her smile immediately dispersed any nerves I was experiencing. I realised, within a minute of speaking to her during the hovering around period just after the collection, that her wry smile was hiding the fact that she had organised the request that I personally attended and it was one of the most successful protests I had seen. The manager overseeing the whole operation even allowed his staff to have a quickie lunch even though the hundreds of staff had foregone their right to a break, the stoppage having gone on so long. Not for the first time during the dispute I was offered a free meal. Roger drove the buckets full of notes and coins with me to the GMB (as he was their branch secretary) and we spent the rest of the afternoon counting and banking with a few volunteers down at the GMB offices.

Chapter 15: My trip to the Inland Revenue

Following the day of action at the end of January 1990, it was clear to any observer that ordinary workers from all walks of life were prepared to take 15, 30, 60 minutes or more as a stoppage from work for us and, in some cases as reported on the national TV news, the whole day of support. We heard from one of our members that he had been contacted by someone at the Inland Revenue and they urgently wanted to speak to the collection officer from the Joint Unions. I thought he was winding me up as he had a habit of "gilding the lily" on occasions, mostly when he opened his mouth. However within a day or so this information was confirmed by far more reliable sources and I was given a 'phone number to ring. I walked the few feet into the forbidden zone of the station forecourt and caught the attention of the officer on duty, Evan Carpenter. Evan was sympathetic and tipped us off to all sorts of golden nuggets and was the unofficial link between the locked out staff at the top of the drive and the Chief and managers at H.Q.

I told him that I needed to use the 'phone and it was important but didn't give him any details. When the response to my: "Hello, I'm ringing from the Ambulance Service, I've been given this number" was "Yes we've been expecting a call" I was shocked. The lady said that I was to make an appointment for the end of the week and report to reception and ask for her. I needed Roger L with me again and I had a fear they wanted the books,that the bank may have bubbled us and I started to try to work out how many laws I may have broken.

I was worried en route and had a vision of being arrested in my uniform and having to take one for the team. On arrival I met with the lady I had spoken with on the telephone and was led up in the lift to the top floor and asked to wait in the lift lobby. A minute or so later she returned and she led me into a room that obviously belonged to the most senior and important tax officer in the country. He smiled and gestured for me to sit down. My tongue at that point cleaved to the roof of my mouth.

I realised that Roger was downstairs with the books in the back of his car and thought at that moment what a stupid decision that was to bring the whole stack of evidence with us to the site. The man (who I won't name) smiled and said in two sentences that he knew that there were substantial amounts of money being collected and neither he nor any of his staff were remotely interested in the tax element of the collection or the payments and wished me luck and said he hoped the dispute would soon be solved.

I almost thought there was a catch but he walked me back to the lift and stepped inside with me. We alighted on the first floor and he walked me to what I could tell from the school dinners smell was the staff canteen. Inside the whole workforce were assembled and burst into spontaneous applause. A union rep from the CPSA approached me and said that they wanted the same sort of address that his colleagues in Companies House had heard the week before. I re-hashed my speech, this time without amplification, throwing in a few nervous jokes that I still thought that I may be arrested any minute. They had even brought their own bucket which was cash full by the end, the members getting up one after the other in an orderly manner to give their donation as I spoke. I felt like a busker.

Chapter 16: The negotiations

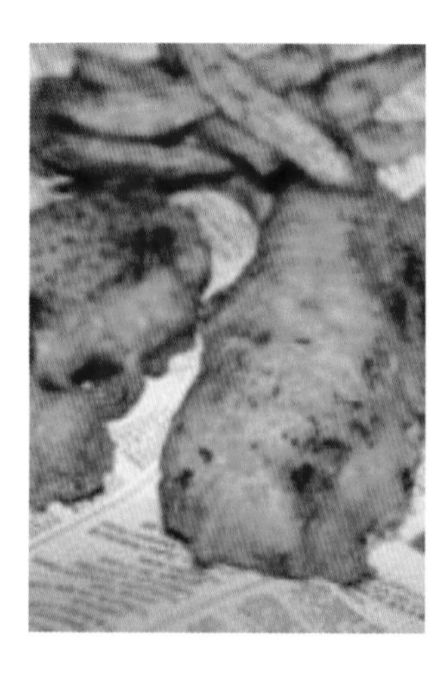

February was torture with press reports of some regions considering wildcat strikes. The pressure to return to work had intensified and the few members of APAP, the non-union body, had started to get restless as they had no official voice. Staff from outlying stations had come to the last couple of meetings and were hyper-critical of both the national and regional reps and full time officers and one or two members said they were giving up.

There had been some issues that had arisen in the press that had started to push our cause off the front pages even though every development was still reported. On 11 February 1990, Nelson Mandela was released from jail in South Africa and the BBC carried live broadcasts of his walk through the gates. There was also intense unease building about the introduction of the poll-tax which started to dominate most news reports.

The dispute breakthrough came with the news that the parties were at ACAS, the arbitration service. The talks took over 20 hours on the first day and the late news reported that they had sent out for chips for them to eat. I knew that was a good sign, as getting to the fish and chip stage reveals progress. The following day they returned for four hours and both sides left upbeat indicating that there would soon be a statement.

Chapter 17: Coach and horses

Throughout the six-month dispute, the unions consistently said there could be no settlement without a pay formula for the future. But at the ACAS office, Roger Poole admitted it had been clear since November 1989 that the Government were not going to grant such a formula. He went on to say however, that the talks had achieved a ``firm framework" for future Whitley Council negotiations. For the first time, the Whitley Council would negotiate ambulance workers' pay without being constrained by any announcement from the Secretary of State for Health before the talks began.

The financial deal was "simply staggering, driving a coach and horses through government pay policy", Roger Poole said. "It goes beyond anything we thought we would achieve when we started this campaign." The value of the deal was then the subject of wildly different interpretations. Roger Poole said that it meant staff would receive 17.6 per cent with an extra 2 per cent available from October, thereby pushing the final figure to 19.6 per cent.

The Department of Health said that as the crews had not received a pay rise since April 1988, the settlement represented 16.9 per cent over three years, with the extra 2 per cent a "target increase" to be awarded locally depending on efficiency improvements.

It was reported that ministers immediately expressed relief that a dispute that caused Government unpopularity appeared to be ending; and the Prime Minister was said to be satisfied by the outcome. Neil Kinnock, the Labour leader of the Opposition, said that the deal had involved concessions by the Government. A good deal had been secured by dint of enormous sacrifice and effective action, he said. But ministers were confident that the firm line taken by the Government, particularly its refusal to concede a pay linkage formula, would serve as a warning to other groups that they would have little to gain by striking.

Despite the sporadic pockets of militancy in some branches that had been reported, union sources stated that they believed the offer would be accepted in the ballot, the result of which was expected by March 13. Some members were nevertheless unhappy that the backdated lump sum payments, ranging from £615 to £915, would not be consolidated into the pay agreement.

The deal meant that a leading ambulance man* now earning £10,888 would receive £11,868 from March, and £12,806 from October. For ambulance men[2]*, the rates would increase from £7,340 to £ 8,001 and then increasing to £8,633 from October. Fully-trained paramedical staff were to receive another £500 per year from April 1st 1990, and partly-trained paramedics between £150 and £230 a year, depending on their skills. This was the first time a payment was ever made for paramedics who qualified with the nationally recognised qualification. [*Within a year the £500 for paramedical skills (as they called it) increased to £600 and was itemised for the benefit of some courses that had modules. The payments were £200 for intubation and infusion (I&I), £200 for Defibrillator and ECG and a further £200 for the carrying of and administration of the drugs.*] The most senior ambulance officers' pay would rise from £16,462 to £19,362.

---

[2] All press reports regarding this settlement used the phrase ambulanceman/men, which were the terms used by the Whitley Council in their communications. The unions were keen to use the generic phrase 'ambulance workers' and regularly used 'ambulance men and women' in communications. Within another five years the Whitley phrase became 'ambulance person'.

The deal also included a new London allowance of £1300 a year for 1989-90 and local pay flexibility with a target increase of no more than 2% from 1st October funded by efficiency savings.

Channel 4 News ran a report the day afterwards and asked Roger Poole and Kenneth Clarke for their views of the other's performance during the dispute. Roger Poole said:

> "I would ask the Secretary of State to improve his performance next year. Let's make sure that we maintain the value of that settlement. If we do, we won't have industrial action again".

Kenneth Clarke said in response

> "I have admired his performance, particularly in the presentation of his case. I look forward to having a drink with him shortly and making sure that we both agree, as obviously we do, that this should not happen again".

Chapter 18: Conclusion

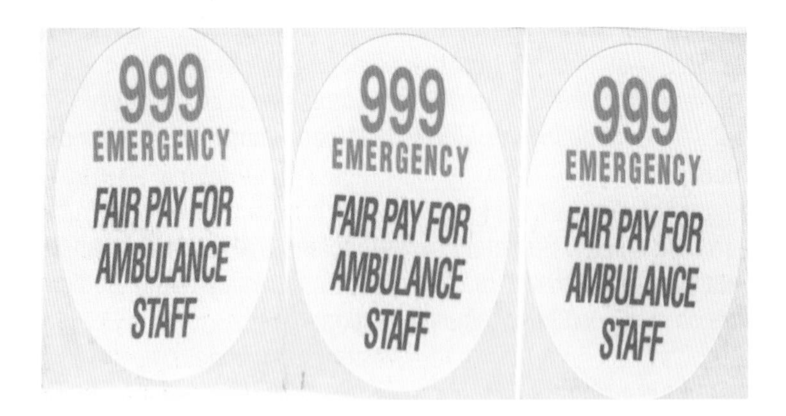

Writing in 2010 I am very conscious of both those who may remember their own stories if they were part of the dispute and still work for the Service or the wider NHS, and those who have memories but have left. I am particularly aware that there are probably over 20,000 staff who have started work in the Ambulance Service since the middle of 1990 and I have worked or spoken with a fair number of them. When the subject of the dispute arises many of them cannot really believe aspects of the story, unimaginable as it would be today.

I am also drawn towards the people who have memories of the dispute who didn't work in the Service - the public. The kindness of those who gave so generously and so often to our collections. The five million people who signed our petition, the first 4.5 million signatures getting it into the Guinness Book of Records as the biggest petition in the world ever. The staff at virtually every fast food restaurant and outlet in the land who gave sandwiches, burgers, coffees and teas (including McDonalds meals) for free every time they saw a collection of ambulance uniforms at that time. The people who had a connection to us be it family working in the NHS or the memory of a relative needing emergency assistance.

In the intervening years, the job and the Service has changed confirming my 20 year cycle theory detailed early in the book. There has been a change in the way Services are run.

Although still within the NHS, they are individual Trusts with Chief Executives and Boards instead of belonging to the Local Health Authority and Departments. Some of them are racing to try and achieve Foundation Trust status, a world away from the "Department within the NHS Status" in which we found ourselves back then in 1989/1990. The Crown badge remains an integral part of the branding of the Service and the Service delivery is still "free" at the point of need, true to the founding NHS principles. We have targets now which are ever harder to achieve even though we have more money allocated per vehicle proportionately than 20 years ago and with increases in demand there has not been the corresponding rise in numbers of staff and vehicles. The issue that brought the dispute to a head and cost me 30% of my wages initially and culminated in the injunction was the practice of skilled emergency personnel undertaking scheduled journeys to routine outpatient appointments. This practice ceased in 1990 as soon as the dispute was over, the management being a little nervous about re-instating it. Some Ambulance Services suffered from becoming NHS Trusts because often the commissioning Hospital Trust would farm routine Services out to the lowest bidder, effectively privatising the outpatients' arm of the service, undercutting the in-house bid. This was quite ironic seeing how "important" to the Service it was in 1989 where there was an insistence that Emergency crews did it instead of the dedicated teams of Patient Transport Services (PTS) staff we had in every corner of the UK. Within the settlement there was provision for 2% extra pay to be awarded locally. Before the wounds of the dispute had even healed, the management enforced a sickness and attendance allowance of the 2% with most staff critical that "taking off" 2% from your wages - even if you caught an illness from a patient - was a reminder of the power management retained, and echoed the 30% cut endured in October 1989.

It took quite some time to fully work in partnership with local and national management after that 2% bump in the road.
The Service has seen the introduction of new roles although they are based around the Paramedic function which is now mainstreamed and a household word. It seems strange now when people still say Ambulance drivers instead of Paramedic even though that is what we are some of the time (drivers of Ambulance vehicles). You never hear the phrase "Fire Engine drivers" or "Police Car drivers". The Ambulance Technician role has advanced and now has treatment options including a range of Intra-muscular drugs, Defibrillator

and Laryngeal masks as well as diagnostic aides such as 12 lead ECG's. Paramedics have become registered with the Health Professionals Council (H.P.C.) and thanks to the weaving and tying together of all the NHS pay and terms and conditions under the scheme known as *Agenda for Change*, we finally have the Pay Review Body that was denied to us at the end of the dispute. The dispute recognised that enhanced skills and qualifications should ensure enhanced pay. The *Agenda for Change* scheme, launched in 2004, re-introduced unsocial hours payments and enhanced overtime rates, finally eradicating all aspects of the problematic 1986 deal. During the Job Evaluation period of assimilating staff onto the new scheme, the banding outcomes of Paramedics - and especially Technicians who work on emergency calls - have been the most fought over and heavily disputed in the whole of the NHS.

I believe that there has been a problem with the bandings in *Agenda for Change* and it doesn't sit well for Technicians to be uncomfortably right at the top of Band 4 and Paramedics in Band 5 as my view is that Technicians should be in Band 5 and the Paramedic role would therefore ultimately be Band 6. I believe in patient care initiatives for Technicians commensurate with band 5 responsibilities but that is the subject of a different book.

There has been a progressive move to what the Service calls the "Front Loaded Model" - essentially far more emphasis on getting an 8 minute response by Paramedic (or Technician) often using Rapid Response Vehicles/Fast Response Vehicles (car) which then wait for the fully staffed Ambulance to transport the patient to the place of definitive care (hospital).

All 999 vehicles carry a defibrillator and all staff are trained to use them, a huge 20 year journey that we could only dream about in 1990. Within about three years of the dispute the Navy blue NATO style jumpers were ditched in favour of the green uniform everyone now recognises instantly. We received more television coverage in the six months of the dispute than in all the previous years from joining fully with the NHS back in 1974. The profile has been ascending ever since even though some staff always felt that they were in the shadow of the Police and Fire Service colleagues. The main change is that the aim to achieve parity with the 5th year fire-fighter and the inclusion of Ambulance as a recognised emergency service not just an essential service have all but been dropped within any type of claim in favour of wider integration into the NHS.

The aim of the dispute was not just about pay, it was also about recognition: a recognition by Government that there had been an erosion of the 1986 deal. We wanted recognition that there needed to be a future pay mechanism to avoid the kind of industrial unrest and consequences we had all warned about and then watched take place as the dispute progressed. Secretly we wanted recognition for the important job that we did and, although it was always muted within Government circles, pretty soon we were overwhelmed by the levels of support that we received almost unconditionally from the public. A key lesson learned was that the level of trust and confidence given to us by the public then must never be taken for granted or jeopardised now in any way. We had hold of a valuable reassurance that the public wouldn't let us fail. Because that support was immeasurable then and still exists today, it is humbling to explain to any person that my job involves representing Ambulance staff.

I grew closer to many of my colleagues during the six months that winter. We had to rely on each other and pull our weight thinking always of others and not just ourselves. We had no choice but to become enterprising and I personally learned more skills informally on the hoof during the dispute than I have on any formal training or course since. I always try and undertake at least one or two courses a year. I had a re-evaluation of the decisions made along the way and there is no doubt that our management then couldn't quite overcome the hurdle of taking the action personally and this I believe clouded their judgement in trying to locally resolve the situation. I admired our Chief Keith Goodall then as an honest man of integrity and in hindsight my respect for him has grown. I think he made one mistake by exacerbating the local dispute starving a Capital city of its emergency cover by serving up the injunction so quickly. However his kindness towards me and insight into the future of the Service he shared with me subsequently mean that as time went on I forgave him that one mistake.
I heard recently that apart from 23 days, he arranged for the pension contributions of all the staff who were locked out to be paid ensuring they didn't have a dent in their settlements when they retired. I will only be able to verify this financially on the day of my retirement but I believe that his kindness shows in this action because it was something that none of us had thought about at the time. After the dispute some of the branch officials locally were a bit worn

out and the dynamic within the local branch was changing. I always paid heed to any advice I received from Roger Wimbush when I started to run the branch and later when we merged branches into UNISON (NUPE, COHSE, NALGO) and then merged again geographically.

One of the consequences of unions working together as one unit as described by Bob Abberley when I interviewed him in February 2010 was that three of the unions in the dispute went on to merge as UNISON just a couple of years later became the biggest public sector union in Europe. Bob also mentioned the welfare fund that is still thriving to this day thanks to some shrewd investment and management of the fund by its committee which has been headed for many years by Maggie Dunn - a person synonymous with the Ambulance Service.

I have concentrated on the issues that affected me and may have resonance with others. I have left out the countless individual instances where crews were approached whilst on the picket line by relatives or bystanders and went to the assistance of patients always saying to themselves “we are not on strike”. I also left out anecdotes that I couldn’t verify even though they contained amazing detail. I cannot write someone else’s story, however I read virtually every newspaper headline either on screen or in the library microfiche projector over a couple of days. I decided to write this book in “real time” starting in October and finishing in March so I could speak to people and start the conversation with “Do you realise it is 20 years exactly since...” and that would trigger a response about that stage of the ambulance dispute. I checked and double checked the chronology with Kevin and Ron, a couple of friends who were colleagues back then. I also recommend what is a definitive analysis of the dispute entitled “Third Among Equals” written in 1990 by Allen Kerr and Sanjit Sachdev who were research officers for NUPE at the time.

I am thoroughly proud that I had a supportive family during this period (I still have). My professional life bled through and permeated into my personal life much more than I ever intended and I think that goes for ambulance staff in general both then and now. The whole family were in the dispute, fiancé, mother, sister all played a role to ensure that I didn’t get stressed and tried hard to understand the issues to be there for me. I have always listened to music as my biggest hobby, it is my life: the mechanics of it, the paraphernalia surrounding it but mostly for the emotion and the place inside that it touches.

Released just a few years before the dispute was "Don't Give Up" by Peter Gabriel and Kate Bush who were then and still are now two of my favourite artists and I was privileged to see both of them (separately) in concert. Whilst I was hypnotised by the bass-line in that song, the lyrics that Peter had written inspired me and others. The song describes the hope that comes from the warmth of a loved one amidst the economic despair from the consequences of the ravages of Thatcher's Britain. My favourite section was:

In this proud land we grew up strong
We were wanted all along
I was taught to fight, taught to win
I never thought I could fail
No fight left or so it seems
I am a man whose dreams have all deserted
I've changed my face, I've changed my name
But no one wants you when you lose
Don't give up
You still have us
Don't give up
We don't need much of anything
Don't give up
'cause somewhere there's a place
Where we belong
Rest your head
You worry too much
It's going to be alright
When times get rough
You can fall back on us
Don't give up
Please don't give up.

I mentioned that the song was uplifting to quite a few colleagues and they all agreed that it had the same effect on them.
I realised that freezing the mortgage in late 1989 added three months to the term, but more than pay and calculations the thing that amazed me was the resilience we demonstrated. We wouldn't starve and neither would our families.

I spent the first few years after the dispute with some bitter feelings that the maelstrom had happened to just some of us whilst colleagues elsewhere didn't really suffer, but as time moved on, so did I and let all of those thoughts evaporate. I realised that there is no one person or group who owns a monopoly on patient care and I have reminded people at all levels that pursuance of common goals and values can only be done together, as when there is a rift and division I feel I know what the consequences could be.

Speaking to friends and colleagues 20 years on I'm surprised at the warmth in memory the responses contain especially when public support is mentioned. I have reminded a few people that it was a cold and stormy winter both outdoors and indoors and I hope I have accurately reflected the environment both political and physical. I too take heart at the overwhelming support the public showed us collectively and individually and that has remained intact.
I'm pleased that I am out the other side far wiser, as it was one of the most significant events in my life. I know why I have had to write my account of these events: it is for me, for the people who were there and especially for the ones who were not. It almost belies belief that these things happened. There is a strange comfort in knowing that we are no longer "Third Amongst Equals", that our standing in the public eye has elevated us to a special place not just as an Emergency Service which we demanded recognition for but within the N.H.S. where we are much more integrated 20 years later.

It is comforting to still be here when the establishment that we were up against in 1989/90 had dug in so deep to be almost untouchable, yet they are mostly all gone and we are mostly all still here. That is reassuring. In its historical context the dispute stands as a watershed in the politics of the UK. Mrs Thatcher is one of the most iconic leaders of the 20th century and there were significant moments in her residence at Number 10, namely the Falklands Conflict and the Miners' Strike prior to the Ambulance Dispute. By the time the dispute ended in February 1990 we were just weeks away from the Poll Tax Riots - considered by most to signal the beginning of her downfall and fall from grace. The ambulance dispute was a pre-curser to the opposition the Government endured in the spring of 1990 following the challenge to her leadership in December 1989.

It was reported that Sir Nicholas Fairbairn admitted there were

> "a number of issues which were causing worries, such as the ambulance dispute, mortgage rates and the poll tax. But these are typical mid-term blues. They are not the stuff of which we are going to change the leader".

She was forced to resign by her own party on 28 November 1990.

Annex 1: Diary of the Dispute

May 1989 National Unions recommend acceptance of 6.5% pay offer

May 1989 Ambulance members vote 3:2 to reject 6.5% offer

July 1989 Rejection confirmed in second ballot by 2:1

September 7th1989 Members vote 4:1 to suspend overtime and working rest days starting Sept 13th offer to suspend action if Govt agree to arbitration

September 22nd 1989 Govt refuse arbitration, peace talks break down

September 29th 1989 Officers and Control staff vote to join overtime ban 4th Oct

October 4th 1989 11 year old letter from Margaret Thatcher unearthed proposing her argument that all 3 Emergency Services to have a pay formula linking pay to national price or wage rises

October 30th 1989 Unions ban non emergency work, reports of Army on standby

November 8th 1989 Army Ambulances on streets of London

November 11th 1989 London Crews Suspended

December 15th 1989 4.5million signature Petition lodged in Parliament

January 13th 1990 National Demonstration 75000 march & rally London

January 30th 1990 National Solidarity lunchtime "Ambulance Support Day"

February 24th 1990 ACAS Talks finalise deal after over 24 hours negotiation

March 16th 1990 Dispute ends following 4:1 vote acceptance of 17.6% overall in Ballot. Return to normal working resumes

Late 1990 Union Loyalty Badges issued

Annex 2: Personalities from the Dispute

Roger Poole
Lead Negotiator NUPE, gradually changed appearance in first few months of dispute becoming more groomed, haircut, obligatory union smart overcoat, briefcase, personable TV manner, West Country accent, articulate, able to coin a phrase at will.

Donna Covey
GMB officer, only female in negotiating team, smartly dressed, attractive, articulate, able to warm up members meetings.

Bob Abberley
COHSE negotiator, officer since 1979, ex operating theatre staff Hereford Hospital, football fan, worked hard behind the scenes politically.

Kenneth Clarke
Secretary of State for Health
MP since 1970, introduced internal market to the NHS, wore suede shoes, liked cigars and jazz, changed his accent from Cambridge days.

Virginia Bottomley
MP since 1984 became Junior Minister of Health in 1989

Ann Widdecombe
Junior Health Minister

Annex 3: Interview with Bob Abberley

February 2010, Central London

Joseph Conaghan. Thanks for seeing me and reading the book
Bob: You've reminded me of some things I had forgotten Joe, I found it hard just to move on whilst reading it as I would remember stories that applied to me from the moments you dwelled on.

J.C. Hopefully that's good, we'll come back to those moments. I'd like to start with the obvious question Win, Lose or Draw...what is your take on the outcome of the dispute?
Bob: When all things are considered I would say draw, although at the time we felt like it was a small victory but history would show a draw. You have to realise that this dispute was unique for many reasons. Firstly it took place in the midst of Maggie Thatcher's period of the most rabid anti Trade Union movement Government that had ever been. Secondly there was an overwhelming high level of public support for you the staff that had never been seen for any group before and for that matter since. Plus there was a completely different approach and execution to this dispute than anything that had previously occurred in the Public Sector, so a draw was quite some result.

J.C. In what sense was the approach different?
Bob: Well there were 5 unions all with membership in Ambulance and each one assigned their lead officer in Health to the dispute at an early stage. Each General Secretary had to agree this was the strategy and it was only to go ahead when they all agreed and they did. As well as Roger from NUPE and myself from COHSE there was Donna Covey from GMB, Danny Bryan from T&GWU and Owen Davies from NALGO although Kevin Greene was in the background and deputised so we were always 5. We united in our approach to the challenges we met every day, we all knew what to say, it wasn't rehearsed but we were all on message. We acted as if we were one union and effectively operated as one unit but as NUPE had the biggest membership Roger became the main spokesperson.

J.C. What was your distinct role amongst the 5 of you?
Bob: Well I was beavering away behind the scenes in Parliament, essentially lobbying MPs to bring them up to speed with the developments as they happened. I realised quite early on that there was not much point lobbying the Labour or Liberals in opposition as they were on side with the Ambulance workers and we needed to get to the influential Tories. It didn't take long before there were quite a few cracks showing within their ranks.

J.C. Which MPs stand out in your memory amongst the Tory ranks as being influential or sympathetic?
Bob: As you can read in one of your Hansard extracts Jerry Hayes was the most vocal of the Conservative group, at one stage I was meeting with him virtually every day. Then there was Peter Holt, Michael Colvin from Romsey and Peter Temple Morris originally from Cardiff and the MP for Leominster who eventually crossed the floor to become a Labour MP some years later. They were putting pressure on the Government to sort out the dispute as they had sensed the mood of their constituents who mostly supported the Ambulance workers. All this pressure was building up within the Conservative party itself.

J.C. You've drifted back to using the phrase "Ambulance Workers" a couple of times Bob, who coined that phrase and how did it get adopted?
Bob: Well Ambulance staff were very resourceful then as now and hard working. For example on the odd day during the dispute I could get home from London (which wasn't often) I would call in at Watford Station on the way. There they had a Head of Collections, a Head of Food, Head of Communications and someone making sure they attended the Station and collecting following their old rota as if they were still on the road and not locked out. I'd often show my face there for a cup of tea night or day, the same went for all of the hotspots. Roger had the main communication role and was the spokesperson and we noticed a good reaction to the phrase. We knew that the public believed that the Ambulance workers wouldn't strike and were annoyed by the way the Employers responded to them by lock-outs, suspensions and injunctions.

We were always representing workers involved in a dispute. When we worked together we always strove for the greater good of the cause so there wasn't much of a personal stamp from anyone as negotiators we worked by committee, the 5 of us acting only for the collective not their individual union. So the answer is we coined it.

J.C. What relationship did you have with the media during the dispute?
Bob: Well the amazing thing looking back was that there was no internet or mobile phones so we relied on the hard work of the press offices at the Union. We would meet every day and agree what would be released. On more than one occasion the media would try and ring us up separately but we were a tight unit and very wise to that tactic. Every press statement or comment aimed at any of the 5 unions was channelled back through us and then articulated through Roger. There were some journalists such as Barrie Clement from *The Independent* who I know you've been in touch with about the book who seemed to have an amazing intuition during the dispute and their reporting was very important. Not a day went by without us all agreeing the story from our end. It was very interesting to then see it reported. It was a well thought out strategy and no union had come across in the public eye as well before.

J.C. What memory from the dispute has stayed with you?
Bob: There are plenty but one clear memory was during Christmas we had organised a massive toy collection for the staff who were locked out like you who had children. There was a huge amount of boxes of toys, clothes and books and they were being stored down at Waterloo where the London Ambulance Service H.Q. is. I remember Eric Roberts from the Sector was there - he was a NUPE rep - and we were organising the distribution of all these presents. The press were there so was a large gathering of Ambulance staff.

There was a bomb scare from some Government buildings down the road - as you're aware they used to be quite regular in those days. Anyway the crews wasted no time in responding even though they were locked out. They just jumped on the vehicles and went, responded. We couldn't have bought better publicity. The same thing happened again when the storm hit at the end of January. It's things like that have stayed with me.

JC. What do you feel is the legacy left by the Dispute?

Bob: It changed things forever. Before the dispute Paramedics were paying for their own training and fundraising and buying defibrillators themselves for their communities. Immediately within the settlement there was a separate payment for Paramedic skills, promises of more UK trained paramedics with a national accreditation replacing the local schemes and the big one - a defib on every vehicle. That led to the promise mostly fulfilled of a Paramedic on every vehicle. That has been achieved. The settlement was about much more than pay, the main legacy is that the standing in the public eye of Ambulance staff became extremely high during the dispute and has remained so equal or better than nurses.

Aside from that there was the setting up of the national fund that would help ambulance staff in times of difficulty and need, that welfare fund is being administered to this day and has helped countless cases.

Annex 4: The main dispute leaflet

Ambulance staff are asking for pay parity with the Fire Service and a similar pay formula.

If we achieve this, ambulance staff would not have to take industrial action again over a national wage claim.

We are asking for our case to be heard at arbitration. If this were agreed we would cancel the industrial action and would accept the results.

Thatcher praises us - why not pay us?

Deal bombing:

'All the emergency services - ambulance,fire, and police - dug together in the rubble knowing there might be another bomb.'
Ambulanceman Peter Cole

Brighton Hotel bombing:

'We were at the scene of the explosion where a whole hotel floor collapsed minutes after we dragged the bodies clear.'
Ambulanceman of the year
Malcolm Woollard

Clapham rail disaster:

'We had the gruesome task of removing five dead and trapped casualties from under the train .... all horribly mutilated.'
Ambulanceman Alan Woods

Ambulance staff, along with their colleagues in the other emergency services, are often the heroes of the many recent tragedies - risking their own lives to save the victims of these disasters.

Their bravery speaks for itself - but the Government refuses to talk to ambulance staff about a proper pay award.

Notes: